LIFE AFTER DEATH
QUESTIONS PEOPLE ASK

JOHN FLADER

Connor Court Publishing

Life After Death: Questions People Ask by John Flader

Published in 2025 by Connor Court Publishing Pty Ltd

Copyright © John Flader 2025

All rights reserved. No part of this book may be reproduced or transmitted in any form or by any means, electronic or mechanical, including photo copying, recording or by any information storage and retrieval system, without prior permission in writing from the publisher.

Connor Court Publishing Pty Ltd

PO Box 7257

Redland Bay QLD 4165

sales@connorcourt.com

www.connorcourtbooks.com

Printed in Australia

ISBN: 9781923224889

Front cover designed by Mathew De Sousa

Bible citations from the The Revised Standard Version, Second Catholic Edition.

Dedicated to all those who have helped me believe in life after death and in the beautiful reality of heaven, in the hope of meeting them there

TABLE OF CONTENTS

Introduction   1

Foreword   3

Death

1. Should the thought of death make us sad?   7
2. Will God forgive sinners at the very end of their life?   9
3. Is there any evidence for life after death?   11
4. Can we trust accounts of near-death experiences?   15
5. What is Pascal's wager about God and life after death?   17
6. Does God predestine some souls to hell and others to heaven?   19

The Particular Judgment

7. What is the particular judgment?   23
8. By what standard will God judge us?   25
9. Will we all be judged differently?   27
10. Should we fear the judgment?   29

Hell

11. Is hell real?   33
12. In what does the suffering of the soul in hell consist?   35
13. What did the ancients believe about hell?   38
14. What do theologians today believe about hell?   40
15. Can we believe there is no one in hell?   41
16. Is it reasonable at least to hope there is no one in hell?   43
17. How could a good God send anyone to hell?   46
18. Can we pray for the souls in hell to be freed from their suffering?   47
19. How is hell compatible with God's mercy?   49
20. If someone commits a mortal sin will he go to hell for it?   51
21. Who was Sr Josefa Menendez, who had revelations of hell?   53
22. What were some of Sr Josefa Menendez's revelations?   55
23. Is it true that Pope Francis once denied the existence of hell?   57
24. Did Christ really descend into hell?   59

Purgatory

25. What is purgatory and why should it exist? 61
26. Is there any evidence for purgatory in the Bible? 64
27. Did they believe in purgatory in the early Church? 66
28. Apparitions of souls in purgatory 68
29. What sort of suffering do souls have in purgatory? 71
30. Are there different degrees of suffering in purgatory? 73
31. Is there time in purgatory? 75
32. Is purgatory somehow a manifestation of God's mercy 77
33. Should we always pray for those who have died? 78
34. What are Gregorian Masses for the faithful departed? 81
35. How do our prayers help the souls in purgatory? 82
36. Can the souls in purgatory pray for us? 84
37. Do souls in purgatory know we are praying for them? 86

Heaven

38. What is heaven like, and might it boring? 89
39. How do we know there is a heaven? 91
40. Where is heaven? 93
41. Is heaven only on earth? 95
42. Can someone be certain of going to heaven? 97
43. Is everyone equally happy in heaven? 99
44. Where did the good people of the Old Testament go when they died? 101
45. Can unbaptised infants go to heaven? 103
46. Can non-Catholics go to heaven? 106
47. Can someone who has left the Catholic Church go to heaven? 108
48. Can atheists go to heaven? 110
49. Do Catholics have any advantage in going to heaven? 112
50. Is there time in heaven? 114
51. Do pets go to heaven? 116
52. Is it easy to go straight to heaven? 118
53. Can we ask Our Lady and the saints in heaven to pray for us? 120
54. Do the saints in heaven feel sad for those in hell? 123
55. Will we be reunited with family members in heaven? 124
56. How old will we be in heaven? 126

57. Will there be disabilities in heaven?	129
58. When did those who died before Christ go to heaven?	130

The Last Day

59. What do we mean when we speak about the Last Day?	133
60. What do we know about the Last Judgment?	135
61. What do we mean by the resurrection of the body?	137
62. Were some of the dead really raised when Christ died on the cross?	140
63. What do we know about the "new heaven and new earth"?	142

Introduction

This book is the fourth in a series on issues of life after death. All of them, the present one included, have been written for non-believers, people who may even reject the notion of continuing existence beyond the grave. The first, *Dying to Live*, was published in 2022 with the aim of giving evidence for the existence of life after death, and showing the reader what to expect in the next life. The second, *The Final Exam*, came out the following year and offers a comprehensive study of the moral life, based entirely on the natural law, to help the reader prepare for the final and most important exam of all: the judgment of the soul before God immediately after death. The third, *From Time to Eternity*, was published in 2024 as a sort of handbook on how to live one's daily life in a busy, materialistic world, without losing sight of the ultimate goal of heaven.

After the last book appeared, people kept asking me whether I was going to write another one. My answer was invariably, "I hope not". It takes a lot of time to write a book and spare time is not one of my long suits. Each of the first three books was helped to come to light by a personal medical condition which prevented me from engaging in various forms of exercise, giving me extra time to write. But I had no such condition when people asked me about a fourth book.

But then it occurred to me that I had already written a large number of articles on all aspects of the next life in my weekly columns in Sydney's *The Catholic Weekly* over the previous twenty years. If there were enough of them, they could constitute a new book, which I would not have to compose from scratch. In fact, I found almost fifty, so that was a start. Looking at the topics, I saw some gaps and so decided to write more articles to plug the gaps and make the book more complete.

So that is how this book came to be. When I started putting it together, I was gifted with another medical condition, which gave me the extra time needed to finish the book in some three months. Sometimes a medical condition can be a real blessing!

The question-and-answer format makes it easy for readers to look at the table of contents and find questions of particular interest to them. Or they can read the book from cover to cover, as usual.

Since these books are addressed to people of all religious persuasions and of none, I have made little reference in them to the Bible and Church teaching. Nonetheless, the last chapters of *Dying to Live* justify looking at what the Church teaches on the afterlife and they use this teaching to explain what we can expect when we die. Given that justification, *From Time to Eternity* has more such references than the first two books, and the present one has still more. I don't apologise for that. The non-religious reader will at least see what the Church teaches, and they are free to accept it or reject it. But since the Church was founded and teaches in the name of Jesus Christ, who showed by his life, miracles and teachings that he was God, what the Church teaches on any question is worthy of at least serious consideration.

Moreover, what is described in this book is not fiction, the flights of fancy of a hyperactive imagination. It is reality. Reality described by Christ and taught by his Church for the last two thousand years. But also, reality as experienced by people in a variety of ways, as this book will make clear. It is a reality we would be foolish to ignore or dismiss altogether. One day we will face it.

We should remember that what happens when we die does not depend on what we think is going to happen. We might think that when we die we will just disappear, never to be seen again. That might not be bad at all. At least we wouldn't have to suffer. Or that we will automatically go straight to that state of everlasting bliss which we call heaven. That would be much nicer. In fact, what happens has more possibilities than these two and it is vitally important to know what they are.

After all, we are all going to die, and knowing what awaits us on the other side can be a big help in using the time which remains to prepare ourselves for it. It is my hope that readers will learn something from this book that will help them live a good life and deserve to spend eternity with God in heaven.

Foreword

In a world now often described as post-Christian we might expect that people would be less and less interested in Christianity, more specifically in the Catholic Church, which has certainly undergone its own exceptionally painful crisis of credibility over the last 25 years or so. Throughout the relatively affluent nations of the world it would be hard to think of an institution so widely assumed in popular culture, in the media, and among the halls of academia and the elites of the intelligentsia to be so irrelevant to the actual realities of daily human life – and also antithetical to what is assumed to be the superiority of modernity.

Yet despite a seeming deepening chasm between modern life and Christianity, the questions about Jesus Christ, God, the Church and the afterlife have obstinately multiplied. In recent years the Church in many countries has experienced significantly higher numbers of people seeking to enter it and to embrace its demanding counter-cultural teachings on sexual morality, marriage and the sanctity of life. At Easter 2025, France was expecting more than 17,000 individuals to enter the Church, more than double the number of the year before. And this in a nation with a deeply entrenched, centuries-old tradition of official secularism dating back to the French Revolution. Similar increases have been reported in numerous other countries.

Whole books can – and probably will – be written on why this trend has begun to occur. Yet it demonstrates that people all over the world are finding something today in the Catholic Church and, more broadly, in the Christian faith, that they cannot find elsewhere in cultures and societies which regard themselves as sophisticated and cosmopolitan, with no need for the ancient 'superstitions' of an 'outdated' religious faith such as Christianity.

In this regard, Dr Flader's latest book of answers to questions that people have asked about life after death is not only timely but also something of a sign of the times. People are hungry for truth, for meaning, for a sense of purpose, for something which offers light to guide them in this world in darkness and gives them hope for a life of happiness both here and hereafter. This book shows them the way and provides spiritual sustenance that overcomes the passing fads and trends of transient modernity as it rushes headlong from one obsession to the next.

Life after Death neatly complements the author's very popular and important titles published in the last few years: *Dying to Live – Reflections on Life after Death*, *The Final Exam – Preparing for the Judgment* and *From Time to Eternity – the Journey to Heaven*. It gives clear answers on what we all wonder about and hope for after that event which we will all face, sometimes with a sense of trepidation – our death.

Two things are important to note here. First, if people increasingly have questions about whether God exists, who Jesus Christ is and what the Church is all about, they will naturally have questions about what the implications are if God actually exists, especially that most important question: Is there life after death? And those many others that follow from this one. Are we really going to face God and give an account of our whole life in a judgment? Does hell really exist and, if so, who goes there? Is heaven as happy a place as they say it is? Is there really a state of purification to prepare the soul for heaven, the state they call purgatory? And what about the final judgment and the resurrection of the body at the end of time?

These are important questions because the answers can have a big impact on how we live our daily lives in preparation for what awaits us when we die. If we kept them in mind on a regular basis and lived our lives accordingly, there is no doubt they would help us to be very well prepared for our definitive encounter with God.

This book is clearly one of the best resources one can find today to answer these and many more questions. Practically every important question people have asked about life after death is answered here. And the questions are answered in the clear, simple style which has characterised the author's writings on matters of faith in his more than twenty years of answering questions each week in various Catholic publications. Not for nothing have his columns been one of the most popular in these publications over the years. As a witness to this, by popular demand they have led to the publication of six volumes of 150 questions and answers each on all matters religious.

The second noteworthy point is that, as readers delve more and more deeply into the pages of this book, they will discover the opposite of what they might expect about a book on the Church's teaching on the afterlife. The book is not some heavy treatise of dogma, but rather an extraordinarily uplifting, inspiring and hope-filled treasure-trove of information about death and eternal life. Just as a student sitting in a classroom on a hot summer day may be bored by a physics lesson, yet astonished when he begins to realise its implications for the Big Bang and the origin of the universe, so the reader of this book will be filled with hope for what awaits us after death. In this light, the answers to questions such as "By what standard will God judge us?" and "How do we know there is a heaven?" are not mere doodling on a page but rather an eye-opener to the extraordinary reality and wonder of the next life. What is more, in these pages the reader will find a God who is not one of wrath, ever ready to punish, but rather one of love and mercy.

This book is – as it should be – a wonderful mixture of deadly seriousness and hope. We need to understand the seriousness of hell. Once we have died, there is no possibility of changing our minds about where we want to go, just because we have ended up in the wrong place. Our judgment by God will occur, whether we want it to or not. Yet more than outweighing the suffering of hell is the wild wonder of heaven, the astonishing love of God and the room in the heavenly mansion that Christ has gone ahead to prepare for us.

Dr Flader's latest book – and long may he continue to produce them – is extremely difficult to put down once the reader picks it up, and it makes an ideal gift for the occasions that often occur in passing encounters or conversations whenever the subject of death and the afterlife come up. Readers will not be disappointed.

Peter Rosengren
Editor, *The Record* (2001-2013)
Editor, *The Catholic Weekly* (2013 – 2023)

Death

1 Should the thought of death make us sad?

I was talking recently with a group of friends at work about a funeral I had just attended and one of my colleagues said she didn't want to talk about death because it makes her sad. What can I tell her to show the beauty of our Catholic understanding of death?

I suspect there are quite a few people who don't want to think about death, let alone talk about it. Why is this? For most it is probably that they focus on the suffering that may accompany dying and then on death as the end of everything, without raising their thoughts to what lies beyond.

How can we help them? To begin with, we should remember that death is a "fact of life" for everyone, absolutely everyone. It is a consequence of original sin and it will come sooner or later to everyone, whether they believe in life after death and in God or not. Not thinking about death is not going to delay or take away its inevitability. In view of that, it makes no sense to avoid considering it and it makes every sense to prepare for it.

For us Christians, death and what follows it have a very positive meaning. Death is not the end of our existence, but only the gateway to eternal life with God. Even Jesus died, to redeem us, and in dying, so to speak, he redeemed death itself. He rose again on the third day and our soul will rise again to eternal life – or of course to eternal damnation if we do not repent of our serious sins before we die. As the *Catechism of the Catholic Church* puts it, "For those who die in Christ's grace it is a participation in the death of the Lord, so that they can also share his Resurrection" (*CCC* 1006).

We should never forget this. After death we can rise up to the indescribable happiness of heaven. "Life is changed, not ended", we say in the first Preface of funeral Masses. But not only is life changed, it is changed for the better, for the very much better. The

Catechism expresses it like this: "Because of Christ, Christian death has a positive meaning: 'For to me to live is Christ, and to die is gain' (*Phil* 1:21). 'The saying is sure: if we have died with him, we will also live with him' (*2 Tim* 2:11)" (*CCC* 1010).

In the same passage in which St Paul says "to die is gain", he goes on to say: "My desire is to depart and be with Christ, for that is far better" (*Phil* 1:23). So too the psalmist speaks of his desire to be with God: "As a deer longs for flowing streams, so longs my soul for you, O God. My soul thirsts for God, for the living God. When shall I come and behold the face of God?" (*Ps* 42:1-2)

This desire for God directs our attention beyond death to what lies ahead for the soul. It does not focus on death but on what comes after it. It takes death for granted and looks forward to the eternal life that follows it. This is how we too should look upon death: not as some sad and unfortunate end, but as the gateway to eternal happiness.

St Cyprian describes death in a beautiful way: "What an honour, what happiness to depart joyfully from this world, to go forth in glory from the anguish and pain, in one moment to close the eyes that looked on the world of men and in the next to open them at once to look on God and Christ! You are suddenly withdrawn from earth to find yourself in the kingdom of heaven" (*Tract. ad Fortunatum*, ch. 13).

And St Ignatius of Antioch, on his way to Rome to be martyred around the year 107, wrote to the Church in Rome:

> All the ends of the earth, all the kingdoms of the world would be of no profit to me; so far as I am concerned, to die in Jesus Christ is better than to be monarch of earth's widest bounds. He who died for us is all that I seek; he who rose again for us is my whole desire... Here and now, as I write in the fullness of life, I am yearning for death with all the passion of a lover. Earthly longings have been crucified; in me there is left no spark of desire for mundane things, but only a murmur of living water that whispers within me, 'Come to the Father' (*Lett. to Romans*, 6, 1-9; 3).

Likewise, St Teresa of Avila writes: "I want to see God and, in order to see him, I must die" (*Life*, ch. 1). And St Thérèse of Lisieux: "I am not dying; I am entering life" (*The Last Conversations*).

What could be more positive and encouraging than this? We are truly blessed to be able to look on death in such a hope-filled way.

2 Will God forgive sinners at the very end of their life?

Will God forgive sinners if they are sorry and ask for forgiveness at the very end of their life? I read somewhere that he will and that even Judas would have been forgiven if he had asked God for mercy. Can you shed some light on this?

The short answer is that God will always forgive sinners, even if it be at the very last moment of their life, provided they are sorry for their sins. But a longer explanation is needed to understand the implications of this.

We can start with what the *Catechism of the Catholic Church* says about it. Speaking about who goes to hell the Catechism says: "To die in mortal sin without repenting and accepting God's merciful love means remaining separated from him for ever by our own free choice. This state of definitive self-exclusion from communion with God and the blessed is called 'hell'" (*CCC* 1033). The implication is that as long as someone in mortal sin repents and accepts God's merciful love, he will be saved, no matter when this is, even at the last moment of his life.

As always, this repentance must be genuine, with a true conversion of heart, even when it comes at the very end of life. As the Catechism puts it, "Interior repentance is a radical reorientation of our whole life, a return, a conversion to God with all our heart, an end of sin, a turning away from evil, with repugnance towards the evil actions we have committed. At the same time it entails the desire and resolution to change one's life, with hope in God's mercy and trust in the help of his grace" (*CCC* 1431). Although the person may not experience all of this, it is clear that repentance must be a real conversion of heart, a rejection of sin, not just a passing thought or sentiment.

How would a person who has lived a life of sin repent at the last moment? It can only be by the grace of God, who moves them to repent. The Catechism explains: "Conversion is first of all a work of the grace of God who makes our hearts return to him: 'Restore us to thyself, O Lord, that we may be restored!' God gives us the strength to begin anew" (*Lam* 5:21; *CCC* 1432).

But conversion must also involve the person's free response to that grace: "It is in discovering the greatness of God's love that our heart is shaken by the horror and weight of sin and begins to fear offending God by sin and being separated from him. The human heart is converted by looking upon him whom our sins have pierced" (*CCC* 1432).

Is it easy for someone who has lived far from God, in some cases in repeated grave sin and even denying belief in God, to repent at the last moment? No, it is not. Their pride and hard heart may often lead them to reject God, even when it means everlasting punishment in hell. Naturally, God always offers them sufficient grace to be saved, but he also respects their freedom to refuse it. This is sad, but it is a necessary consequence of human freedom.

Does God actually give a hardened sinner this grace at the very last moment of their life? We can never know for certain, but it is most likely that the answer is yes. After all, he "desires all men to be saved and to come to the knowledge of the truth" (*1 Tim* 2:4). He will stop at nothing to rescue sinners from eternal damnation. He is ever rich in mercy. He is the good shepherd who goes in search of the lost sheep (cf. *Luke* 15:3-7) and who lays down his life for his sheep (cf. *John* 10:11). He is the Son of man, who came "to give his life as a ransom for many" (*Matthew* 20:28). "So it is not the will of my Father who is in heaven that one of these little ones should perish" (*Matthew* 18:12-14). As confirmation of this, there are numerous examples of people who had lived far from God but had big conversions at the end of their life and were well prepared to go to heaven.

Two final thoughts on the question. First, we should pray very much for those we know who are living far from God so that God will grant them the grace of repentance, and we should do all we can to help them humanly: talking with them, giving them good books and articles to read, inviting them to speak with a priest, etc. Second, after someone like this has died in apparent rejection of God, we should continue praying for them, since they may have been saved at the last moment and are now atoning for their many sins in purgatory. We should never assume that anyone has gone to hell. After all, to pray for the living and the dead is one of the spiritual works of mercy.

3 Is there any evidence for life after death?

A work colleague has recently been diagnosed with terminal cancer and I was talking with him about what happens after he dies. He says he doesn't believe in life after death. How can I convince him that there is?

Unfortunately, there are many people who think like your colleague – that with death all is ended and there is nothing afterwards. They sometimes say that no one has ever come back from the dead to tell us about it, and this confirms them in their belief. How do we answer them? It is not enough to say that Jesus spoke about eternal life, or that we believe in it. They want hard evidence, even if, as Jesus said, "neither will they be convinced if some one should rise from the dead" (*Luke* 16:31). Let us consider a few facts which may, or may not, convince the sceptic.

A first argument comes from the very nature of the human person, composed of a material body and a spiritual soul. What is the soul? It is the spiritual element of the human person, by which we think, plan for the future, know immaterial objects and ideas such as God, love, honesty, etc. With our soul we can also love, desire and freely choose to do this or that. We can write books and compose symphonies. And, very importantly, because we have a spiritual soul, we can make progress, from making tools and planting crops to building skyscrapers, airplanes and computers, and curing illnesses. Animals cannot do these things, because they do not have a spiritual soul.

The soul is clearly distinct from the body even though it is intimately united to it as long as we live. When we die, the body decays but the soul, being spiritual, cannot decay or be destroyed. It lives on necessarily. While by reason alone we cannot know what happens to the soul after we die, we can know that it must necessarily continue in existence. Through revelation we know what does happen to the soul after death: it goes to heaven or hell, or to purgatory as the antechamber of heaven.

A second argument is the fact that people have in fact come back from the dead and appeared on earth, among them Mary, the mother of Jesus. Her apparitions at Fatima, Portugal, to three small children aged 10, 9 and 7 each month from May through October 1917 are perhaps the most convincing, because Our Lady made a prophecy there that came true several months later. In the July apparition she told the children that in October she would work a miracle that all would see. On October 13 some 70,000 people trudged through the rain and mud in the hope of seeing the miracle. Although it had been raining steadily, suddenly the clouds parted and the sun appeared. It began to revolve, sending out rays of light of different colours that lit up the surroundings and then it seemed to fall from the sky towards the people, who fell on their knees and begged God for mercy. To their great relief the sun returned to its place. All those present and some in the surrounding villages saw the miracle. Even sceptics reported seeing it and anti-clerical newspapers in Lisbon wrote articles on it. The fulfilment of the prophecy in such a dramatic way can only be explained if Mary did in fact come back to earth to prophesy the miracle, which then happened on the day she announced.

A third argument for life after death comes from the many cases of near-death experiences, in which people died clinically while their soul left the body and went into another world where they encountered people who had died. A particularly well known and convincing case is that of a three-year-old boy named Colton Burpo from Nebraska, U.S.A. It was popularised in the book and later the film *Heaven is for Real*. While undergoing surgery in 2003, Colton appeared to have died, but meanwhile his soul went to heaven and he was later able to describe events he could not possibly have known about in life. He spoke of meeting his unborn sister, who had been miscarried by his mother and who told him her name. He also met and recognised his great-grandfather, who had died thirty years before Colton was born. This could not be attributed to his imagination, since he did not know he had an unborn sister and the description he gave of his great-grandfather, whom he had never known, was accurate and could only have come from having seen him in the next life.

A fourth type of evidence for life after death is the appearance on earth of souls in purgatory. There are numerous books which relate these apparitions. I will use just one recent one, *Hungry Souls* (TAN Books, Charlotte 2012) by Dutch psychotherapist Gerard van den Aardweg. The author relates what he saw in the church of the Sacred Heart of Suffrage near the Vatican in Rome, where there are exhibits of ten artifacts related to appearances of souls in purgatory, all of them involving burn marks.

One is a clearly visible burn mark of the right hand of a Benedictine choir sister named Clara Schoelers, who had died of the plague in 1637 and appeared to Maria Herendorps, a lay sister in the Benedictine monastery of Vinenberg, near Warendorf, Germany, on 13 October 1696. The burn mark is on Herendorps' apron and there are other imprints of both hands on a piece of linen.

Another burn mark left by a soul in purgatory is in the shrine of the Black Madonna in Czestochowa, Poland. Kept there since the nineteenth century is a corporal, the square linen cloth over which the Body and Blood are consecrated in a Catholic Mass, with the mark of a hand burned through several layers of the folded cloth. It seems that two priests of the Pauline Fathers, who look after the shrine, had promised each other that the one who died first would give the other some sign of life after death. One of them had been dead for a long time without sending any sign and the other was thinking about it at the end of Mass one day as he was folding the corporal, into the customary nine layers. Doubt came over him as to whether there really was life after death, when suddenly a burning hand appeared and scorched the corporal, leaving burn marks on many layers of the cloth. The hand then disappeared.

There is no way to explain the burn marks of a human hand produced in such a remarkable way except by acknowledging that the person whose hand it was had come from life beyond the grave. And of course that the person was somehow on fire. These accounts are attested to by reliable witnesses and are authenticated by Church authorities only after careful examination.

Apparitions from souls in hell are far less common but they too exist. Van den Aardweg relates two such apparitions taken from the book *Hell*, written by Mgr Louis-Gaston de Ségur of Saint-Denis (Paris) in 1876. The first one involved someone from Mgr de Ségur's own family and it took place in Moscow a short time before the bitter military campaign of 1812. Mgr de Ségur's maternal grandfather, Count Rostopchine, Military Governor of Moscow, was a close friend of another general, Count Orloff, a convinced atheist. One day, after a big meal and many drinks, Count Orloff and one of his friends, identified as General V., also an atheist, began ridiculing religion and especially hell. When Count Orloff suggested the possibility of life after death, General V. proposed that whichever of them died first should come back and give word of it to the other. Orloff readily accepted the suggestion.

Some weeks later General V. was sent to the battlefront to engage Napoleon's army. He had been gone two or three weeks when suddenly early one morning Count Orloff burst into Count Rostopchine's room in his dressing gown, visibly disturbed. He explained that a half hour before he was lying in bed when suddenly the curtains of the bed parted and General V. appeared in front of him, standing upright and pale with his hand on his chest. He said: "There is a hell and I am there!" Then he disappeared. Ten or twelve days later word came to Count Rostopchine that General V had been killed by a bullet to his chest. It was at the very hour General

V. appeared to Count Orloff.

Is there life after death? One would be very foolish not to believe it. Very foolish indeed. So, as Christians we live in the hope of eternal life and, when someone is dying, we console them with this hope, helping them to prepare for eternity with God. The thought of death does not frighten us. Rather it fills us with the desire to be with God and to enjoy the "supreme, definitive happiness" which is heaven, as the *Catechism of the Catholic Church* explains (*CCC* 1024).

4 Can we trust accounts of near-death experiences?

We often read of people who have seemingly died and then come back to life, who relate what they saw before they recovered. Can we take these accounts as credible evidence of life after death?

Near-death experiences, in which a person is clinically dead and the soul leaves the body and experiences various stages of the afterlife, are very personal and can be considered something akin to private revelations. As such, they need not be believed by others, and they should be judged carefully on the merits of each one. Some are clearly more credible than others.

Since even canonised saints have had visions of heaven, hell and purgatory, and some have had near-death experiences, we certainly cannot reject them out of hand. One example is that of St Josemaría Escrivá. On 27 April 1954, having suffered from a severe case of diabetes for ten years, he was given a new dose of insulin. He suddenly collapsed and appeared to have died. After ten minutes, he regained consciousness and was thereafter completely cured of the diabetes, something which is medically inexplicable. While he lay there, he saw his whole life pass by very quickly, as if in a film, and he was able to ask God to forgive his failings.

There are literally thousands of people who have reported near-death experiences, people of all ages, of all religions and of none, of all nationalities. Among the most well-known cases are those of

Dr Eben Alexander and Dr Gloria Polo.

Dr Alexander, a neurosurgeon who has taught at various universities, including Harvard Medical School, is the author of the best-selling book *Proof of Heaven: A Neurosurgeon's Journey into the Afterlife*, published in 2012. In it he relates how in 2008, while in an induced coma after suffering meningitis, he found himself in a state where he experienced what we would call heaven, and he encountered God. Before that experience he could not reconcile his knowledge of neuroscience with belief in God, heaven or even the soul as something different from the brain. His experience completely transformed him, moving him to write his book. Today he believes that true health can only be achieved when we acknowledge that God and the soul are real, and that death is not the end of our existence, but only the passage into a different form of life.

Dr Gloria Polo is a Colombian orthodontist, whose life was transformed radically when she was struck by lightning in May 1995 while walking on the campus of the National University of Bogotá with her 23-year old nephew. He was killed instantly and Gloria went into cardiac arrest, her body badly burned, inside and out. Although she had been attending Sunday Mass, she had not been to confession since she was thirteen, she was using an intrauterine device for contraception, she had had an abortion and had paid for others to have them, and she was living a very materialistic, self-centered and ungodly life. What is more, she had told others that devils do not exist and even that God did not exist.

While her body lay on the operating table, she began to see devils coming after her and she found herself falling down a tunnel into hell, with people young and old screaming in pain and grinding their teeth. She saw that the sins that condemned her most included aiding and participating in abortion, receiving holy communion in a state of mortal sin, fortune-telling, and speaking badly of priests.

In that state, she also saw the great suffering of the souls in purgatory, including that of her parents. Then she passed through a beautiful tunnel of light to a place of great joy and peace where she was able to embrace her deceased relatives. She also experienced her own judgment, seeing her whole life played out as in a movie with all her actions, good and bad, and their consequences. She understood how God regards sexual immorality, abortion and methods of contraception that cause abortions, as well as how he looked on her materialism, her excessive concern for what she wore and how she looked, and her lack of faith.

She was given a second chance in order to amend her ways and to tell others what she had experienced. She has written her account in the book *Struck by Lightning: Death, Judgement and Conversion*. While we are not required by the Church to believe accounts such as these, common sense tells us that we would be very foolish to dismiss them.

5 What is Pascal's wager about God and life after death?

I remember hearing once about an argument for living as if there were life after death called Pascal's wager. Can you enlighten me as to exactly what this argument is, as I have a friend who doesn't believe in life after death?

Pascal's wager comes from Blaise Pascal (1623-1662), the famous French mathematician, physicist, inventor and philosopher. The wager comes in his posthumously published *Pensées*, or *Thoughts*, in Part III, Section 233. It is intended to show that it is better to wager that there is a God and therefore life after death, and to live one's life in accordance with that belief, than to bet that there is no God and no life after death. A summary of the wager goes like this.

Either there is a God or there is not. Pascal says that reason cannot decide between the two. That is, we cannot know by reason alone whether there is a God. It should be said, contrary to this statement of Pascal, that human reason can show that there is a God, starting with arguments presented by Aristotle and St Thomas Aquinas and, more recently, with arguments from the cosmos. But let us continue with Pascal's argument.

We can consider human life then like a game, in which at the end there is a God and life after death or there is not. It is like tossing a coin, which will come up heads or tails. Heads means there is a God, and you live happily with him forever after in indescribable bliss. Tails means there is no God and your life comes to an end. You must wager; you must decide how you are going to live. It is not optional.

In fact, we could add, people do wager. Many believe in God and try to live in accordance with his commandments, telling him they are sorry when they fail and starting over. Others, relatively few, bet there is no God and don't worry about God's laws, although they try not to get caught by the laws of men. Some of these, nonetheless, "hedge their bets" and endeavour to live a decent life "just in case".

Let us first consider the consequences if we bet that there is a God and life after death. If we win and there is a God, we gain everything. We bet the finite life we live on earth and we gain union with God in heaven for all eternity. If we lose and there is no God, we lose nothing. We simply cease to exist after living a good life here on earth. So, betting on God offers the chance to gain everything and lose nothing.

Alternatively, we can bet that there is no God and live our life accordingly: in self-indulgence, dishonesty, pride, etc. If we win and there is no God, we gain nothing, for there was nothing to gain. We simply cease to exist. But if we lose and there is a God, we miss out on the infinite reward of eternal life with him in heaven. We lose everything. And of course, although Pascal doesn't say it, this implies suffering for all eternity in hell.

It is clear from this argument that it would be foolish indeed to bet that there is no God. There is nothing to gain and everything to lose, whereas betting that there is a God promises everything to gain and nothing to lose.

But there is more to it than what awaits us after death. Pascal does not mention this, but it is important to consider that those who live a good life here on earth find great happiness already in this life. They will fail often, as we all do, but the very effort to be kind, generous, honest, hard-working, loyal, brings its own reward. The psalm says it all: "Blessed are those whose ways are blameless, who walk in the law of the Lord" (*Ps* 119:1).

Conversely, those who disregard God's law and the good of others may make a lot of money and have many possessions, but they do not have the peace of mind, the joy of life that the others do. As C.S. Lewis says in his book *The Great Divorce,* which is an allegory on heaven and hell, those who go to heaven begin their heaven on earth and those who go to hell begin their hell on earth.

So, independently of what awaits us in the next life, already in this life we reap the rewards of betting that there is a God and life after death and living in accordance with that belief. And if we bet that there is no God we suffer in this life as well as in the next.

It is clear which is the better wager.

6 Does God predestine some souls to hell and others to heaven?

I was recently reading St Paul's letter to the Romans, where he talks about predestination. Does God really predestine some souls to heaven and others to hell? If so, to what extent are we still free to work out our own destiny? I am really confused.

The passage to which you refer reads: "We know that in everything God works for good with those who love him, who are called according to his purpose. For those whom he foreknew he also predestined to be conformed to the image of his Son, in order that he might be the first-born among many brethren. And those whom he predestined he also called; and those whom he called he also justified, and those whom he justified he also glorified" (*Rom* 8:29-30).

So, St Paul does indeed speak of predestination. But to what extent does it affect a free person? Are there some people whom God has predestined to heaven, and they will go there no matter how many sins they commit, even if they remain unrepentant when they die? And are there others whom God predestined to hell, and there is nothing they can do to avoid it? When expressed like this, the thought of predestination is truly frightening. It makes a mockery of human freedom and personal merit for the good deeds we do, or the punishment we deserve for our sins. And it makes a mockery too of God's mercy and justice.

Fortunately, that is not how we are to understand predestination. *The Catholic Encyclopedia* explains it: "Predestination, taken in its widest meaning, is every divine decree by which God, owing to his infallible prescience of the future, has appointed and ordained from eternity all events occurring in time, especially those which directly proceed from, or at least are influenced by, man's free will." In other words, God's plan of predestination takes into account the free acts of man, which he foresees from all eternity.

In understanding how predestination relates to human freedom, we must situate it within four fundamental premises or presuppositions. The first is that God wants all to be saved, both Christians and non-Christians. St Paul, in his first letter to Timothy, speaks of "God our Saviour, who desires all men to be saved and to come to the knowledge of the truth" (*1 Tim* 2:4). St Peter writes in a similar vein, saying that God "is forbearing toward you, not wishing that any should perish, but that all should reach repentance" (*2 Pet* 3:9). So, God does not predestine anyone to hell. The *Catechism of the Catholic Church* says as much: "God predestines no one to go to hell; for this a wilful turning away from God (a mortal sin) is necessary, and persistence in it until the end" (*CCC* 1037).

The second premise is that God grants everyone sufficient grace to be saved. This follows from the first premise, and it leads St Augustine to say: "One must not despair of even the greatest sinner as long as he lives here on earth" (*Retract.* I, 19, 7). The Second Vatican Council says, with respect to the salvation of those who do not know God: "Nor shall divine providence deny the assistance necessary for salvation to those who, without any fault of theirs, have not yet arrived at an explicit knowledge of God, and who, not without grace, strive to lead a good life" (*LG* 16).

The third premise is that our good deeds and the merit deriving from them are already the fruit of the grace God has predestined to grant us beforehand. The Catechism says: "The merit of man before God in the Christian life arises from the fact that God has freely chosen to associate man with the work of his grace. The fatherly action of God is first on his own initiative, and then follows man's free acting through his collaboration, so that the merit of good works is to be attributed in the first place to the grace of God, and then to the faithful" (*CCC* 2008).

At the same time, and this is the fourth premise, God grants us this grace, foreseeing that we will correspond to it. The Catechism says that when God "establishes his eternal plan of 'predestination' he includes in it each person's free response to his grace" (*CCC* 600). That is, God grants us his grace, knowing that we will use it to do good deeds deserving of eternal life.

The question of predestination, even taking into account these four premises, still remains in some sense a mystery. But in the end, God is free to bestow his grace and love on whomever he chooses, and he does give everyone sufficient grace to be saved.

The Particular Judgment

7 What is the particular judgment?

I know that when we die we will face God in the judgment. Does the Church have any teaching about the nature, or content, of this judgment?

We should clarify at the outset that when we refer to the judgment of each soul immediately after death, we are speaking of what the Church traditionally calls the particular judgment, the judgment of each soul individually. This judgment is distinguished from the general judgment, the judgment of all souls together on the Last Day.

We can begin with Scripture, where we find a good number of passages that refer to the judgment of each soul after its death. For example, the letter to the Hebrews says: "It is appointed for men to die once, and after that comes judgment" (*Heb* 9:27). And St Paul, in his second letter to the Corinthians, says: "For we must all appear before the judgment seat of Christ, so that each one may receive good or evil, according to what he has done in the body" (*2 Cor* 5:10).

On the basis of these texts and of a constant tradition of the Church, the Catechism teaches: "Each man receives his eternal retribution in his immortal soul at the very moment of his death, in a particular judgment that refers his life to Christ: either entrance into the blessedness of heaven – through a purification or immediately, – or immediate and everlasting damnation" (*CCC* 1022).

The judgment is a crucial moment in our life. It is definitive. On it depends our eternal destiny: either heaven, immediately or via purgatory, or hell. It is truly the "final exam" of our life, as I titled my book *The Final Exam*, (Connor Court 2023). It is the one exam we cannot afford to fail.

At the judgment, there is no opportunity for repenting, or for pleading with God for more time. If we have made bad choices, we have had our whole life to repent and change our ways. With death, our eternal destiny has been decided. St Jerome writes: "What will happen to all on the day of judgment, has already taken place for each one on the day of their death" (*In Joel*, 2:1).

The Catechism teaches: "Death puts an end to human life as the time open to either accepting or rejecting the divine grace manifested in Christ. The New Testament … repeatedly affirms that each will be rewarded immediately after death in accordance with his works and faith" (*CCC* 1021).

St Paul may be describing the judgment when he compares being judged by others with being judged by God: "But with me it is a very small thing that I should be judged by you or by any human court. I do not even judge myself. I am not aware of anything against myself, but I am not thereby acquitted. It is the Lord who judges me. Therefore, do not pronounce judgment before the time, before the Lord comes, who will bring to light the things now hidden in darkness and will disclose the purposes of the heart. Then every man will receive his commendation from God" (*1 Cor* 4:3-5).

St Paul is saying that when he examines his conduct, his conscience is clear, but that does not justify him before God. It is God who will judge him. What is more, God will bring to light things hidden in darkness, things or deeds we have forgotten about completely, both good and bad. And he will reveal the purposes, the motives, that moved us to do what we did.

All of this is telling us that the particular judgment will be thorough, complete, objective. We will not be able to hide anything. All will be brought to light. And we will not be able to come with excuses, to justify our conduct. We will accept what we see, because we will acknowledge that, before God, it is the truth. We will see ourselves as God sees us, not as we see ourselves.

As I wrote in *Dying to Live* (Connor Court 2022), in the numerous accounts of near-death experiences, all those who found themselves in the particular judgment as deserving of hell acknowledged that that is what they deserved for their sins. If they had excuses when they committed those sins, there was no place for excuses now.

This teaching is an invitation to live well and to repent of our sins, now, while there is still time.

8 By what standard will God judge us?

When people of different religions and of none have such different ideas of what is right and wrong, how is God going to judge them? What standard can he use so that his judgment is fair?

That is a very good question. As you say, in today's world there are big differences in how people see the morality of acts, even in such basic ones as abortion, euthanasia, homosexual acts, etc.

Looking at it from another point of view, there are those who say that the question of what is right and wrong is completely subjective. It is relative to how you see it personally in your circumstances. Morality is what you make of it. To each, his own. This is what is known as moral relativism. On the other hand, there are others who say no, that morality is objective, the same for everyone. Independently of how you see it, certain acts are in themselves simply wrong and not to be done, and others are right and good.

How is God going to judge all these people? Will it be by what they think is right and wrong and how they have lived in accordance with their beliefs, or by some other, objective standard?

When we think about it, we would probably hope and expect that God would judge everyone by the same objective standard. It just doesn't seem right that, if we have made an effort all our life to refrain from doing what we knew was wrong, like being dishonest or greedy, we would receive the same judgment and reward as someone who thought it was okay to be dishonest and greedy and lived accordingly. This, we think, would simply not be fair.

Or, looking at it in another way, if someone thinks it is quite okay to steal my outdoor furniture or my car, to kill my daughter or to sleep with my wife, I would not say he is entitled to his opinion – to each his own. No, after all, some actions are just plain wrong, no matter what people may think. They are wrong always and everywhere.

Ancient philosophers like Aristotle, who lived in the fourth century before Christ, Cicero, who followed him three centuries later, and many others found an objective standard of morality in human nature. The word nature, by the way, refers to what makes something to be what it is and not something else. So trees have tree nature, horses have horse nature and humans have human nature.

When we reflect on human nature, as the philosophers have done, we see that acts like stealing, fraud, killing an innocent person, etc., are contrary to the good of the individual and of society, and so they are simply wrong. This is what has come to be called the natural law, because it is based on human nature. So much is this recognised universally that every society has laws which punish acts like these. Since everyone is deemed to be aware of these basic principles, God can judge everyone by this same objective standard.

Although everyone is deemed to know the fundamental principles of the natural law, there are other principles of which some people may be ignorant. Some people were simply never told that acts like the use of contraception to prevent pregnancy, sexual acts by oneself or with another outside of marriage, homosexual acts, etc., are wrong.

As we all know, in order to commit a serious sin, one of the conditions is that we must have full knowledge that the act is seriously sinful. If someone is ignorant of this through no fault of their own, they are not held accountable for a serious sin before

God. Therefore, in the particular judgment too, God will not hold them responsible for those acts. God is just, and merciful, and he will not punish someone for something they did not know was wrong.

But since sin always hurts the sinner, and often others as well, we should make every effort to learn the principles of God's law, so that we can live well and not be found wanting in the judgment. For those who want to learn the Church's teaching, the *Catechism of the Catholic Church* has a very complete treatment of moral life, and my book *The Final Exam* is a simplified commentary on it, based wholly on the natural law.

9 Will we all be judged differently?

It doesn't seem fair to me that someone who grew up in a dysfunctional family without any religion should, in the judgment by God, be judged the same as someone from a loving family where they practised their faith regularly. Am I right in this?

I think we would all agree that such a judgment would not be fair. Since God is all wise, just and merciful, he will surely take into account every aspect of our background and life, and will judge each person accordingly.

Let us consider two very different scenarios. In the first case the person was born into a family where their mother and father were united in marriage, they prayed together and went to church on Sundays, and the children grew up in a climate of generosity and love, where they were taught what was right and wrong and learned to practise the virtues. That helped them live a good moral life and use their talents for the benefit of others.

Another person was born into a single-parent family without any religious upbringing, where they experienced a lack of love, arguments, alcohol or drug abuse, domestic violence and so on. Later in life they had no religious faith, became involved in drugs and stealing, and had a series of broken relationships. It is obvious that God will not expect as much from the second person as from the first. That is only right.

Other aspects of life too have a bearing on how we live and how God will judge us. Consider the various talents we have received: intelligence, an out-going personality, an even temper, the opportunity to attend a good school or university, etc. God can expect more from a person with more such talents than from someone with fewer.

Or the responsibilities that different people have. Bishops and priests will have to render an account for how they used their ministry for the benefit of the people in their care, doing all they could to help them go to heaven. For this reason, we should pray very much for them when God calls them to himself. And parents will answer for how they formed their children in virtues and faith, helping them to be saints so that they in turn can help many others go to heaven.

It is obvious that, because God is fair, he will judge each person in accordance with the gifts he has received. We see this in Christ's parable of the talents, where one person was given five talents, another two and another one. It is an image of God giving different opportunities and abilities to each person and judging them according to how they used them. In the parable, the first person traded with his five talents and made five more, the second made two more and the third buried his talent in order not to lose it and he returned it to his master.

In the final reckoning the first two heard the words, "Well done, good and faithful servant; you have been faithful over a little, I will set you over much; enter into the joy of your master." The one who had not used his one talent to good advantage was told, "You wicked and slothful servant! You knew that I reap where I have not sowed, and gather where I have not winnowed? Then you ought to have invested my money with the bankers, and at my coming I should have received what was my own with interest. So take the talent from him, and give it to him who has the ten talents. For to every one who has will more be given, and he will have abundance;

but from him who has not, even what he has will be taken away" (*Matt* 25:14-29).

We see this too in that other familiar statement: "Every one to whom much is given, of him will much be required" (*Luke* 12:48).

In the judgment, what God expects is that we use well the gifts and talents he has given us, whether few or many, not that we achieve what someone with more talents does. God is fair, he is just. And of course he is always merciful too.

10 Should we fear the judgment?

I sometimes fear that God's judgment will be harsh because, after all, he is God and perhaps he expects much more from me than I think. Are my fears founded?

We should never fear being judged by God. He is our Father, and he loves us more than we love ourselves. He wants us to be with him forever in heaven, not separated from him in hell. As St Paul writes, Jesus wants all to be saved and to come to the knowledge of the truth (cf. *1 Tim* 2:4). What is more, to help us live well and deserve to go to heaven, God gives us abundant graces throughout our life, including the grace of forgiving our sins every time we tell him we are sorry. He is just and fair, as we have seen, but he is also merciful. He is the father of the prodigal son, who celebrates with open arms the return of his repentant son (cf. *Luke* 15:11-24).

What is more, it is Jesus himself who will be our judge. He says so: "The Father judges no one, but has given all judgment to the Son, that all may honour the Son, even as they honour the Father… Truly, truly, I say to you, the hour is coming, and now is, when the dead will hear the voice of the Son of God, and those who hear will live. For as the Father has life in himself, so he has granted the Son also to have life in himself, and has given him authority to execute judgment, because he is the Son of man" (*John* 5:22-23, 25-27).

Yes, Jesus, the Son of man, will be our judge. He often called himself the Son of man, a title that goes back to the Old Testament. As he was born of Mary, he is truly man, truly human, and so he knows our human nature, with all its weaknesses. It is thus consoling to know that we will be judged by one who is human like us, as well as being, of course, God, the second Person of the Blessed Trinity.

A very revealing experience of the judgment is related by Dr Raymond Moody in his book on near-death experiences *The Light Beyond* (Rider, UK, 2005). It concerns a man who was living a criminal life when he was struck by lightning on the golf course and "died". He had a near-death experience in which he passed through a tunnel into a bright pastoral setting where he met a being of light whom he called "God", who led him through a life review. In it, he relived his entire life, not only seeing his actions but feeling their effects on others. The experience changed him completely for the better (pp. 33-34).

This man did not speak of fear or dread in the judgment, even though he had been living a very sinful life. He spoke rather of a peaceful, loving God, who showed him heaven where he would go if he repented. Feeling the effects of his actions on others in the judgment is an experience that a good number of people who have had near-death experiences relate. It must be very sobering to feel what others have felt as a result of our actions, whether good or bad.

What we too will experience in the judgment is a loving God, who knows us better than we know ourselves. He knows everything about us, our thoughts as well as our actions. We read in the book of Psalms: "O Lord, you have searched me and known me! You know when I sit and when I rise up; you discern my thoughts from afar. You search out my path and my lying down, and are acquainted with all my ways. Even before a word is on my tongue, behold, O Lord, you know it altogether… You know me right well" (*Ps* 139:1-4, 14). In another passage we read: "The Lord sees not as man sees; man looks on the outward appearance, but the Lord looks on the heart" (*1 Sam* 16:7).

This is a great consolation for us. While others, who see only our outward behaviour, sometimes misjudge us and attribute to us motives we never had, God knows us completely. He knows our true motives, our intentions, and he will judge us fairly.

So we should never fear the judgment. What we should do is strive to be very sincere with ourselves, avoid sinning as much as we can and do much good, telling God often that we are sorry for our sins because they offend him. Then we can look forward to the judgment with great hope and peace.

Hell

11 Is hell real?

How do I help someone who knows what the Church teaches on hell but who doubts whether there really is such a place?

To answer your question we should first remind ourselves of what Christ and the Church teach about hell. Jesus Christ spoke about hell numerous times. In his description of the judgment he speaks of the Son of man coming in his glory and gathering before him all the nations, separating them as the shepherd separates the sheep from the goats. After describing the reward of eternal life to be given to the righteous, he says to the others: "Depart from me, you cursed, into the eternal fire prepared for the devil and his angels; for I was hungry and you gave me no food, I was thirsty and you gave me no drink... And they will go away into eternal punishment, but the righteous into eternal life" (*Matt* 25:31-46).

We find the teaching of the Church in the Catechism: "The teaching of the Church affirms the existence of hell and its eternity. Immediately after death the souls of those who die in a state of mortal sin descend into hell, where they suffer the punishments of hell, 'eternal fire'. The chief punishment of hell is eternal separation from God, in whom alone man can possess the life and happiness for which he was created and for which he longs" (*CCC* 1035).

Returning to your question, when someone is sceptical about an aspect of the faith for which there is no immediate evidence, it is often difficult to convince them, no matter what arguments or "proofs" we use. We recall Our Lord's parable of the rich man and Lazarus, in which the rich man, now in hell, begs Abraham to send Lazarus to his father's house to speak with his five brothers, lest they go to hell too. Abraham answers: "'They have Moses and the prophets; let them hear them.' And he said, 'No, father Abraham; but if someone goes to them from the dead, they will repent.' He said to him, 'If they do not hear Moses and the prophets, neither will they be convinced if some one should rise from the dead'" (*Luke* 16:19-31). So we cannot expect the sceptics to believe in hell even if we tell them that Christ and the Church taught its existence. Nor if we tell them that people alive today have actually seen it.

We have already seen, in question 4, the experience of Gloria Polo, the Colombian orthodontist who was struck by lightning in 1995 and, while apparently dead, was shown her judgment in which she was condemned to hell and was taken there to see it. Another person is Sr Josefa Menendez, a Spanish nun who died in 1923. She was taken to hell numerous times and describes in her book *The Way of Divine Love* the excruciating pain she suffered and the cries of hatred and despair of the damned souls she saw there. Likewise, the three children at Fatima saw a vision of hell, which they described as a sea of fire with demons and lost souls shrieking and groaning with sorrow and despair.

As we saw in question 3, Dutch psychologist Gerard van den Aardweg relates two accounts of apparitions from hell in his book *Hungry Souls*. We have already seen the first one, involving two Russian generals who scoffed at religion and denied the existence of hell. One of them was killed in battle and appeared to the other from hell, confirming its existence.

When Bishop de Ségur, who relates the accounts in his book *Hell*, told this story to the Superior of a religious community in 1859, the latter related another story told to him by a relative of the woman protagonist, who was then still alive. This woman, at the time a widow of about twenty-nine years of age, was in London in the winter of 1847 to 1848. She was very worldly, wealthy and attractive, and was sinning with a young man. One night around one in the morning, as she was falling asleep, a glimmer of light appeared at the door of her room and it gradually became brighter and larger. Then she saw the door open slowly. It was the young man, who entered and came over to her. He took her by the left wrist and said, "There is a hell." The pain in her wrist was so great that she passed out.

A half hour later she came to and called for her chambermaid, who noticed the smell of burning when she entered the room. She looked at the woman's wrist and saw a burn mark the size of a man's hand so deep that the bone was laid bare. What is more, the carpet was burned with the imprint of a man's steps from the door to the bed and back again. The next day the woman learned that the man had died at the very time he appeared to her. After that the woman wore a broad gold bracelet to cover the burn mark.

So there is a hell. We can pray for all those we know who are living far from God so that they repent and do not go there. Perhaps our prayers will save them.

12 In what does the suffering of the soul in hell consist?

Can you tell me something about the suffering of souls in hell? Also, how can a spiritual soul suffer from fire when it doesn't have a body?

The two principal forms of suffering of souls in hell are eternal separation from God and eternal fire.

As regards the separation, the Catechism teaches: "The chief punishment of hell is eternal separation from God, in whom alone man can possess the life and happiness for which he was created and for which he longs" (*CCC* 1035). This is easy to understand. We naturally desire happiness and we find the greatest happiness when we find the greatest good, who is God himself, the infinite good. For this reason St Augustine writes: "You have made us for yourself, and our heart is restless until it rests in you" (*Conf.* 1, 1, 1).

Even though many people do not believe in God, they naturally desire him because they want to be happy. To be eternally separated from the one Being who can make us truly happy is therefore the greatest of suffering.

The other punishment is, of course, eternal fire. Jesus himself speaks of it numerous times. For example, describing the last judgment, he says of those who have not loved him with deeds:

"Depart from me, you cursed, into the eternal fire prepared for the devil and his angels…" (*Matt* 25:41). If we consider the intensity of the pain of being burned by fire here on earth, we cannot begin to imagine the pain of the fire of hell. And it is forever.

If we ask how a spiritual soul can suffer from corporeal fire, we need only remind ourselves of Jesus' words that the fire of hell was prepared for the devil and his angels. Devils are pure spirits and yet they can suffer from this fire. If they can, so can human souls.

St Thomas Aquinas explains in the Supplement to his *Summa Theologiae* why this punishment is fitting: "Further, punishment should correspond to sin. Now in sinning the soul subjected itself to the body by sinful concupiscence. Therefore, it is just that it should be punished by being made subject to a bodily thing by suffering therefrom" (*STh*, Suppl., q. 70, art. 3). The "bodily thing" is the fire.

Although these are the two principal forms of suffering, there are others. St Catherine of Siena records in her *Dialogue* these words from God himself:

> In hell the souls have four principal torments, out of which proceed all the other torments. The *first* is that they see themselves deprived of the vision of me, which is such pain to them that, were it possible, they would rather choose the fire, and the tortures and torments and to see me than to be without the torments and not to see me.
>
> This first pain revives in them, then, the *second*, the worm of conscience, which gnaws unceasingly, seeing that the soul is deprived of me, and of the conversation of the angels, through her sin, made worthy of the conversation and sight of the devils, which vision of the devil is the *third* pain and redoubles to them their every toil… And the sight is more painful to them, because they see him in his own form, which is so horrible that the heart of man could not imagine it…
>
> The *fourth* torment they have is the fire. This fire burns and does not consume, for the being of the soul cannot be consumed, because it is not a material thing that fire can consume. But I, by divine justice, have permitted the fire to

burn them with torments, so that it torments them, without consuming them, with the greatest pains in diverse ways according to the diversity of their sins, to some more, and to some less, according to the gravity of their fault. Out of these four torments issue all the others, such as cold and heat and gnashing of the teeth and many others (*Dialogue*, Ch. 2).

St John Chrysostom comments on the pains of hell: "It is true that the pain of hell is unbearable. But if someone were capable of imagining 10,000 hells, the suffering would be nothing compared to the pain of having lost heaven and of being rejected by Christ" (*Catena Aurea*, vol. 1).

Another form of suffering in hell is loneliness. The souls there have no concern for one another, for they are completely wrapped up in themselves. Fr Gabriele Amorth, an exorcist for the diocese of Rome, relates the following story:

One day Father Candido [an exorcist] asked a thirteen-year-old girl, "Two enemies, who hated each other all their lives, hated each other to death, and both ended up in hell. What is the relationship that they will share now, since they will be with each other for all eternity?" And this was the answer [from the devil within her]: "How stupid you are! Down there everyone lives folded within himself and torn apart by his regrets. There is no relationship with anyone; everyone finds himself in the most profound solitude and desperately weeps for the evil that he has committed. It is like a cemetery" (*An exorcist tells his story*, Ignatius Press, San Francisco 1999, p, 76).

Although knowing about these punishments of the soul in hell can be daunting and even frightening, it is at the same time exceedingly helpful. The knowledge of what awaits us in hell if we reject God and die in mortal sin is a powerful incentive to love God more and to lead a good life, so that we do not go to hell ourselves. A young man once told me: "The only thing that prevented me from committing that sin was the fear of hell". What should move us is not fear of hell but love for God. But if love is lacking, thank God for fear of hell.

13 What did the ancients believe about hell?

Some time ago you mentioned that there are contemporary writers who argue that we can hope that no one goes to hell, arguments that quite frankly don't convince me. Did the Fathers of the Church and other early writers have anything to say about this?

Cardinal Avery Dulles, in an excellent article entitled "The Population of Hell" in the May 2003 issue of *First Things*, examined the question at length, speaking not only about early writers but also about contemporary ones. Here I will write about the early views and later about contemporary ones.

Early writers based themselves especially on the Scriptures, in which Jesus spoke often about hell, using expressions like "everlasting fire", "outer darkness" and "weeping and gnashing of teeth". Such was the strength of his teaching that someone once asked him if those to be saved would be only few. He replied, "Strive to enter by the narrow door; for many, I tell you, will seek to enter and not be able (*Luke* 13:23-24). On another occasion he said, "Many are called, but few are chosen" (*Matt* 22:14).

Other texts of the New Testament too speak clearly of the reality of hell. St Peter writes: "If the righteous man is scarcely to be saved, where will the impious and sinner appear?" (*1 Pet* 4:18). And the book of *Revelation* teaches that there is a fiery pit where Satan and those who follow him will be tormented forever: "As for the cowardly, the faithless, the polluted, as for murderers, fornicators, sorcerers, idolaters, and all liars, their lot shall be the lake that burns with fire and brimstone, which is the second death" (*Rev* 21:8).

As regards particular individuals who may be in hell, Cardinal Dulles argues that Jesus' words suggest strongly that the apostle Judas must have been damned. Jesus says that he has kept all those whom the Father has given him except the son of perdition (cf. *John* 17:12), and he even calls Judas a devil (cf. *John* 6:70). On another occasion he says of him: "It would be better for that man if he had never been born" (*Matt* 26:24; *Mark* 14:21). If Judas were among the saved, Dulles argues, these statements could hardly be true. Many saints and Doctors of the Church, among them St Augustine and St Thomas Aquinas, regard it as a revealed truth that Judas went to hell. What is more, the first Eucharistic Prayer of the Mass does not mention the name of Judas when it lists all the other apostles.

What is more, the constant teaching of the Church supports the idea that there are two classes of people after death: the saved and the damned. The Ecumenical Councils of Lyons I (1245), Lyons II (1274) and Florence (1439) all teach this, as do the Bull *Benedictus Deus* of Pope Benedict XII (1336) and the *Catechism of the Catholic Church* (cf. *CCC* 1022 and 1035).

The Church has never defined the question of the relative numbers of those saved and damned. The majority of the Eastern Fathers, among them Saints Irenaeus, Basil and Cyril of Jerusalem, taught that the majority were damned. St John Chrysostom went so far as to say: "Among thousands of people there are not a hundred who will arrive at their salvation, and I am not even certain of that number, so much perversity is there among the young and so much negligence among the old."

St Augustine, who may be taken as representative of the western Fathers, argues too that more are lost than saved. In Book 21 of his *City of God* he denies first that all human beings are saved, then that all the baptised are saved, then that all baptised Catholics are saved, and finally that all baptised Catholics who persevere in the faith are saved. He seems to limit salvation to baptised believers who refrain from serious sin or who, after sinning, repent and are reconciled with God.

At the same time, a few Eastern writers, among them St Clement of Alexandria, St Gregory Nazianzen, St Gregory of Nyssa and Origen sometimes speak as though in the end all are saved. Nonetheless, Origen's views on this question were condemned in a local Council in Constantinople convened by the Emperor Justinian in the year 563.

The great Scholastics of the Middle Ages, among them St Thomas Aquinas, are of the view that relatively few are saved, as are the theologians of the later centuries, among them Francisco Suarez, St Peter Canisius and St Robert Bellarmine in the sixteenth century. In summary, the consensus of early writers is that not only are not all saved, but that more are lost than are saved.

14 What do theologians today believe about hell?

Are there any theologians at the present time who have addressed the question of whether there are many or few souls in hell?

As we have seen, Cardinal Avery Dulles, in his excellent article "The Population of Hell" in the May 2003 issue of *First Things*, spoke not only about early writers but also about contemporary ones. As we recall, the majority of writers up to the sixteenth century taught that more people go to hell than to heaven. There were a few, however, who did believe that everyone might be saved.

It is in the middle of the twentieth century that the view that possibly no one is in hell once again appears. Among its principal exponents is the Jesuit Fr Karl Rahner. He says that Jesus' words on hell appear to be rather warnings than predictions. While allowing for the real possibility of eternal damnation, Rahner says that we must at the same time maintain "the truth of the omnipotence of the universal salvific will of God, the redemption of all by Christ, the duty of men to hope for salvation." Rahner therefore believes that universal salvation is a possibility.

Another proponent of that possibility is the theologian Hans Urs von Balthasar. In his book *Dare We Hope That All Men Be Saved?* he says that we have a right and even a duty to *hope* for the salvation of all, because it is not impossible that even the worst sinners may be moved by God's grace to repent before they die. At the same time, he concedes that since we are able to reject God's grace, we cannot be sure of salvation and we should think of the danger in which we stand. Although Cardinal Dulles regards von Balthasar's position as at least not contrary to Catholic teaching, he mentions that a number of theologians have been very critical of it. Among them are Fathers Jean Galot, Michael Hull and Regis

Scanlon.

Interestingly, von Balthasar quotes a passage from St Teresa Benedicta of the Cross, Edith Stein. She says that since God's all-merciful love descends upon everyone, it is probable that this love produces transforming effects in their lives. To the extent that people open themselves to that love, they enter into the realm of redemption. On this ground St Teresa Benedicta finds it possible to hope that God's omnipotent love finds ways, so to speak, of outwitting human resistance.

Pope St John Paul II, in his book *Crossing the Threshold of Hope*, mentions the theory of von Balthasar. After posing the question of whether a loving God can allow any human being to be condemned to eternal torment, the Pope replies: "And yet the words of Christ are unequivocal. In Matthew's Gospel he speaks clearly of those who will go to eternal punishment (cf. *Matt* 25:46)." As justification for this assessment the Pope asks whether God, who is ultimate justice, can tolerate terrible crimes and let them go unpunished. Final punishment, he says, would seem to be necessary to reestablish the moral equilibrium in the complex history of humanity. Indeed, in view of the terrible atrocities committed at the time of the Second World War and since then, these words of Pope John Paul make much sense.

In summary, down the ages there have been different views on the question of whether there is anyone in hell. The majority, from the Fathers of the Church to the present, have taught that in view of human freedom there will be some, perhaps many, who are not saved. And even those who argue for universal salvation tend to be cautious and limit themselves only to holding out hope that all are saved. As for us, if we struggle to do God's will and repent when we fall, we need have no fear of hell, and rather we can look forward to eternal life in heaven.

15 Can we believe there is no one in hell?

Someone recently told me that David Bentley Hart argues that there is no one in hell and that all are saved. This sounded extreme to me. Can we maintain this position?

The book you mention is *That All Shall Be Saved: Heaven, Hell, and Universal Salvation*, published in 2019. The author was raised an Anglican, converted to Eastern Orthodoxy at the age of twenty-one and is now a research scholar at the University of Notre Dame in the U.S. In this book he maintains that the salvation of all is something that one may not only be hopeful about, as proposed by Karl Rahner, Karl Barth and Hans Urs von Balthasar among others, but that it is absolutely certain. Yes, he says, all are saved. All. From a reasonable point of view this position is untenable.

A recent comprehensive defence of the traditional Christian teaching on the question comes in fellow-theologian Michael McClymond's monumental two-volume work *The Devil's Redemption: A New History and Interpretation of Christian Universalism*, published by Baker Academic in 2018. Universalism, by the way, is the idea that all are saved, with no one in hell.

McClymond says in an article on Hart's book: "His work is a personal statement of 214 pages, without footnotes or source citations, and with minimal reference to the complex historical debates over universalism. My work runs to 1,325 pages, cites more than 3,000 sources, and contains some 3,500 footnotes." Anyone interested in going deeper into this question should read McClymond's book.

McClymond says that in 2015, when he was engaged in email exchanges with Hart over universalism, he told Hart that "the overwhelming majority (perhaps 10-to-1) of the early Christian authors – Greek, Latin, Syriac, and Coptic – were not universalists. In an email response, David wrote that he was more concerned with truth itself than with precedent or authority – though he believed that at least some authorities supported his views. He added that if an eternal hell were a necessary part of Christian teaching, then for him this would mean that Christianity itself would be self-evidently false."

This statement of Hart is truly extraordinary, given that Christ himself often spoke of hell and its eternity. For example, "And they [the damned] will go away into eternal punishment" (*Matt* 25:46). Christ spoke too of the "unquenchable fire" (*Mark* 9:44; 9:48). What is more, the *Catechism of the Catholic Church* states categorically: "The teaching of the Church affirms the existence of hell and its eternity" (*CCC* 1035).

As I wrote in *Question Time 4*, question 484, the Church has always taught that not all are saved. In 1547 the Council of Trent, in its Decree on Justification, solemnly declared: "Although it is true that 'He died for all' (*2 Cor* 5:15), not all, however, receive the benefit of his death, but only those to whom the merit of his Passion is communicated" (*Dz* 795). And in 1549, Pope Pius II condemned the proposition that "all Christians must be saved" (*Dz* 717b). St Peter gives the justification for this teaching: "If the righteous man is scarcely to be saved, where will the impious and sinner appear?" (*1 Pet* 4:18).

Once again, we can quote Cardinal Joseph Ratzinger's statement that God does not force anyone to be saved, so that "God's all-embracing desire to save people does not involve the actual salvation of all men".

Finally, as we have seen, the majority of Fathers of the Church taught that most souls were damned, as did later thinkers like St Thomas Aquinas, Francisco Suarez, St Peter Canisius and St Robert Bellarmine. This is a far cry from arguing that all are saved.

16 Is it reasonable at least to hope there is no one in hell?

After all that has been written on the topic, is it reasonable at least to hope that all will be saved, so that there is no one in hell?

We can start with Jesus' own teaching. We know he spoke about the existence of hell more than seventy times, warning his listeners to be on guard. For example, in his description of the Last Judgment he speaks of the Son of man coming in his glory for the final judgment and saying to those on his left hand: "Depart from me, you cursed, into the eternal fire prepared for the devil and his angels; for I was hungry and you gave me no food, I was thirsty and you gave me no drink... And they will go away into eternal punishment, but the righteous into eternal life" (*Matt* 25:31-46).

He also spoke about how difficult it is to be saved and how easy to be damned: "Enter by the narrow gate; for the gate is wide and the way is easy, that leads to destruction, and those who enter by it are many. For the gate is narrow and the way is hard, that leads to life, and those who find it are few" (*Matt* 7:13-14). His listeners clearly understood that it is not easy to be saved, to a point where someone once asked him: "Lord, will those who are saved be few?" He answered, "Strive to enter by the narrow door..." (*Luke* 13:23-24).

Today the situation is very different. Given the widespread notion that hell does not even exist or, if it does, God's mercy is so great that few people, if any, go there, people would probably rephrase the question: "Lord, will those who go to hell be only a few?"

From the very fact of Jesus' repeated teaching, we can be certain that there is a hell. Jesus, who is full of mercy and wants all to be saved (cf. *1 Tim* 2:4) would not warn people about a state after death that did not exist, or to which no one was going to go. Precisely because he loves us so much and wants all to be with him, he warned us about the real possibility of hell so that we would live good lives, repent of our sins and not have to go there.

Common sense and experience confirm the real possibility of souls going to hell. Given the effects of original sin such as pride, self-centredness, laziness, dishonesty, self-indulgence, etc., we know well that unless we struggle to resist temptations and to do good, it is very easy to lapse into a way of life that is grievously sinful and offensive to God. We know people who have wandered off the path and now lead lives of grave sin, saying they don't believe in God or in life after death and consequently do not pray. This number is constantly growing as fewer people practise the religion in which they grew up and increasing numbers say they do not believe in

God. As a result, serious sin is all around us. It is true that anyone can repent on their deathbed, but we cannot be sure that many will actually do it. Hell is thus a very real possibility for many.

We remember too the declaration of the Second Vatican Council: "Since we know neither the day nor the hour, we should follow the advice of the Lord and watch constantly so that, when the single course of our earthly life is completed, we may merit to enter with him into the marriage feast and be numbered among the blessed and not, like the wicked and slothful servants, be ordered to depart into the eternal fire, into the outer darkness where men will weep and gnash their teeth" (*LG* 48).

What is more, there are numerous people down the ages – among them St Teresa of Avila, Sr Josefa Menendez and the three children of Fatima – who had visions of hell, all speaking of the horrible shrieks and groans of the many people who are there along with the devils. Not to mention that many people who, in near-death experiences, saw the hell to which they would have gone had they not repented.

On the basis of this tradition, Ralph Martin, a consultor to the Pontifical Council for the New Evangelisation, in his book *Will Many be Saved?*, argues strongly against the idea of universal salvation, as do Fathers Jean Galot, Michael Hull, Regis Scanlon and James T. O'Connor.

In summary, we are all free to decide for ourselves whether we think there may be no one in hell. But on the evidence of Scripture, tradition, the teaching of the Church and the testimony of those who have seen hell, this position is most unreasonable, most unlikely to be true. As for me, while I too pray that all will be saved, I firmly believe that, in spite of God's infinite mercy and because of his respect for our freedom, there are many people who will not be saved. And so I will continue to believe, and to teach others, that there is a hell. But at the same time, if we strive to love God with our whole heart and to do his will, repenting of our sins, praying and receiving the sacraments, there is very little likelihood that we will go there ourselves.

17 How could a good God send anyone to hell?

Can you please explain how a good God could send anyone to eternal damnation in hell?

The answer is simple. God doesn't send anyone to hell. Rather, he wants all to be saved and to come to the knowledge of the truth (cf. *1 Tim* 2:4), and he gives everyone sufficient grace to be saved (cf. *2 Cor* 12:9). It is the person who sends himself or herself to hell. The Catechism explains: "To die in mortal sin without repenting and accepting God's merciful love means remaining separated from him for ever by our own free choice. This state of definitive self-exclusion from communion with God and the blessed is called 'hell'" (*CCC* 1033).

Yes, if we do not repent of our sins and accept God's overwhelming, merciful love, we have only ourselves to blame. We remain separated from him by our own free choice. C.S. Lewis, in his book *The Great Divorce*, said practically the same thing some fifty years before the Catechism was written: "There are only two kinds of people in the end: those who say to God, 'Thy will be done' and those to whom God says, in the end, 'Thy will be done.' All that are in hell choose it. No soul that seriously and constantly desires joy will ever miss it. Those who seek find. To those who knock, it is opened" (p. 58).

St John Vianney, the Curé of Ars, in his catechesis, puts it graphically:

> My children, if you saw a man prepare a great pile of wood, heaping up fagots one upon another, and when you asked him what he was doing, he were to answer you, "I am preparing the fire that is to burn me", what would you think? And if you saw this same man set fire to the pile, and when it was lighted throw himself upon it, what would you say? This is what we do when we commit sin. It is not God who casts us into hell; we cast ourselves into it by our sins. The lost souls will say, "I have lost God, my soul, and heaven; it is through my fault, through my fault, through my most grievous fault!" He will raise himself out of the fire only to fall back into it.

He will always feel the desire of rising because he was created for God, the greatest, the highest of beings, the Most High ... as a bird shut up in a room flies to the ceiling, and falls down again, the justice of God is the ceiling which keeps down the lost (*Catechesis 14*, on sin).

But couldn't God take everyone to heaven if he wanted? He could. But it would mean not respecting the freedom he gave us, and God is too much of a father to do that. The then Cardinal Ratzinger, later Pope Benedict XVI, explains:

God never, in any case, forces anyone to be saved. God accepts man's freedom. He is no magician, who will in the end wipe out everything that has happened and wheel out his happy ending. He is a true father; a creator who assents to freedom, even when it is used to reject him. That is why God's all-embracing desire to save people does not involve the actual salvation of all men. He allows us the power to refuse. God loves us; we need only to summon up the humility to allow ourselves to be loved (*God is Near Us*, Ignatius 2003, pp. 36-37).

If we make use of the graces God gives us through his Church, if we struggle to avoid sin and go frequently to the sacraments of the Eucharist and Penance, we can be very confident of going to heaven. And we do very well to remind others of these important truths.

18 Can we pray for the souls in hell to be freed from their suffering?

Would I be wasting my time or even sinning in praying for the souls in hell so that their pain may stop, for example that after a long time they would just burn away and cease to exist?

I understand perfectly your compassion for those souls, but I have to say that there is no point in praying for them. The teaching of Our Lord and his Church is that the punishment of hell is everlasting. Jesus himself says, "Depart from me, you cursed, into the eternal fire prepared for the devil and his angels; for I was hungry and you gave me no food, I was thirsty and you gave me no drink... And they will go away into eternal punishment, but the righteous into eternal life" (*Matt* 25:31-46). Based on this and many other passages in which Jesus speaks of everlasting punishment, the Church has always taught the eternity of hell. For example, the *Catechism of the Catholic Church* says, "The teaching of the Church affirms the existence of hell and its eternity" (*CCC* 1035).

It is difficult to grasp the concept, let alone the reality, of a soul having to suffer for ever with no hope of reprieve. And, moreover, having to suffer a punishment worse than any pain we can suffer on earth. We are inclined to ask how God in his mercy could possibly condemn anyone to such suffering. The answer is of course that God does not want any soul to have to suffer like this. Rather he "desires all men to be saved and to come to the knowledge of the truth" (*1 Tim* 2:4). And, already in the Old Testament, "As I live, says the Lord God, I have no pleasure in the death of the wicked, but that the wicked turn from his way and live" (*Ezek* 33:11).

In the final choice that each person makes before dying, he or she understands that that choice binds the soul forever, that there is no turning back. In a similar way, the bad angels understood clearly that if they turned against God, they would be separated from him forever. It is an awesome moment in the life of a person, the moment in which they decide their eternal destiny, choosing eternal life and joy with God or eternal separation from him and suffering.

Some obvious conclusions suggest themselves. First, we can never know whether an individual person went to hell. The Church, through the process of beatification and canonisation, has declared that many persons are in heaven, but it never declares that anyone is in hell. Therefore, when someone dies who we know has lived a life of sin, we should always pray for them. They may very well have repented just before they died and have avoided hell.

As regards souls who are in hell, we cannot help them. They have chosen that state by their lack of final repentance and our prayers cannot be of benefit to them. We would not be sinning in praying for them, but our prayers would not help them either.

As regards ourselves, if we want to avoid going to hell, and we certainly do, we should live our lives close to God at all times. We should struggle to grow in love for him by doing his will, receiving the sacraments regularly and repenting and turning back to him through the sacrament of Penance when we fail. In that way, we will grow in love for God and we will not reject him at the end of our life.

And finally, we should pray very much for all the people who are presently separated from God through serious sin, especially those whom we know. Our prayers can help them repent so that they do not go to hell. This was a thought that moved the three children at Fatima very much and it led them to offer up generous penances for sinners.

19 How is hell compatible with God's mercy?

I can't imagine how God, who is most merciful, could allow anyone to suffer the pains of hell. Can you help me?

God, who is ever rich in mercy, could not have done more to love us and prevent souls from going to hell. We see this in the Old Testament, where he reveals his avid desire to forgive sinners:

If a wicked man turns away from all the sins which he has committed and keeps all my statutes and does what is lawful and right, he shall surely live; he shall not die. None of the transgressions which he has committed shall be remembered against him; for the righteousness which he has done he shall live. Have I any pleasure in the death of the wicked, says the Lord God, and not rather that he should turn from his way and live? (*Ezek* 18:21-23).

When heaven was closed as a consequence of the original sin of Adam and Eve, God showed his mercy by sending his eternal Son to become man and die on the cross to redeem us and open heaven again: "For God so loved the world that he gave his only-begotten Son, that whoever believes in him should not perish but have eternal life. For God sent the Son into the world, not to condemn the world, but that the world might be saved through him" (*John* 3:16-17).

The depth of God's mercy is seen in the horrific suffering of Jesus Christ in his passion and death on the cross for the salvation of all. "Greater love has no man than this, that a man lay down his life for his friends" (*John* 15:13).

We see it too in the very fact that Jesus spoke often about hell, so that there would be no doubt about the punishment that awaits the unrepentant sinner. That very revelation is a big help to us all when we are tempted to sin.

Jesus shows his great mercy in giving us the seven sacraments, which strengthen us in grace so that we find it easier to keep the commandments and grow in holiness. Among these sacraments is the very sacrament of mercy, the sacrament of Penance. God will forgive us through this sacrament every time we come back to him repentant of our sins. He will have forgiven us hundreds, even thousands, of times through this sacrament by the time we die. That is mercy.

The parable of the lost sheep and the joy of the shepherd in bringing it back is another manifestation of God's mercy. After giving the parable, Jesus comments: "I tell you, there will be more joy in heaven over one sinner who repents than over ninety-nine righteous persons who need no repentance" (*Luke* 15:7). Especially powerful is the parable of the prodigal son, where the sinful son is welcomed back by his father with embraces and kisses, the best robe and a ring, and finally a banquet: "For this my son was dead and is alive again; he was lost, and is found" (*Luke* 15:24). The father is an image of God, the most merciful Father.

If a person commits numerous serious sins throughout his life and is moved to be sorry for them at the very last moment, even on his deathbed, God will always forgive him. As we have seen, St Paul writes that God "desires all men to be saved and to come to the knowledge of the truth" (*1 Tim* 2:4).

God shows his mercy even in the punishment of hell in that the souls there do not suffer all that their sins deserve. If we consider that our sins offend the infinite love and goodness of God, we can understand that an eternity of suffering would be insufficient to make up for even one serious sin. So God, in his mercy, allows the souls in hell to suffer much less than their sins deserve. St Catherine of Genoa writes in *Fire of Love* (Sophia Institute Press 1996): "For the man who is dead in sin merits infinite pain for an infinite time, but God's mercy has allotted infinity to him only in time and has limited the quantity of his pain; in justice God could have given him more pain" (p. 3). Venerable Luis of Granada writes in the same vein. Addressing himself to God, he says:

> Not only your hatred of evil reveals your goodness but even the eternal punishment of hell which you have prepared for the wicked. According to human judgment, the most terrifying thing about hell is that a temporal fault is punished with eternal pain and suffering. The truth of the matter is, however, that even then the fault is not sufficiently punished. But you, Lord, are an abyss of mercy and as you are liberal in rewarding, so also are you clement in punishing, for your reward is greater than our merits and your punishments are less than our sins deserve.
>
> But how can it be that a punishment so terrible and so protracted as that of hell can be considered not only just but even too short and hardly enough for a temporal fault? The reason is that your goodness is so great that a sin committed against it is not fittingly punished even by eternal torment. So great is your goodness, Lord, that no punishment could ever suffice to atone for sins committed against you (*Summa of the Christian Life*, vol. 1, pp. 61-62).

20 If someone commits a mortal sin will he go to hell for it?

Does the very fact of having committed mortal sins mean that the sinner will necessarily go to hell?

I think a good number of people ask this question, fearful that if they have committed mortal sins they will be deserving of hell.

The answer is of course no, mortal sins of themselves do not send a person to hell, as long as the person repents and is sorry for the sins when he comes to the judgment. If mortal sins automatically sent people to hell, hell would be full and few people would go to heaven.

The Catechism is clear on teaching that only the person who does not repent of his mortal sins will go to hell: "To die in mortal sin without repenting and accepting God's merciful love means remaining separated from him for ever by our own free choice. This state of definitive self-exclusion from communion with God and the blessed is called 'hell'" (*CCC* 1033).

God is always merciful, and he wants us to be with him forever in heaven. Indeed, he wants all to be saved. He wants his house in heaven to be full. All we have to do to be saved is to repent sincerely of our sins, and God in his mercy will welcome us home.

Naturally, our sorrow must be genuine, with a true conversion of heart. This implies that we are resolved to do all we can to avoid falling into the same sins again, even though we know that, in our weakness, we may very well fall again. As the Catechism puts it, contrition is "sorrow of the soul and detestation for the sin committed, together with the resolution not to sin again" (*CCC* 1451). For example, we must be prepared to remove any near occasions of the sins we have committed.

We can understand this if we consider how earthly parents will always forgive their children who have done something wrong but come back sincerely sorry. They are understanding when, after the children say they are sorry, they go back and do the same thing again. And again. After all, parents know themselves and they know how often they have been sorry for something but have gone out and done it again. Mind you, it is not that we are creating God in our own image and likeness, making him out to be like us but only much better. He made us in *his* image and likeness and he shares with us a heart capable of loving and forgiving. Again and again.

If we come before God with true sorrow, he will always forgive us and welcome us back with great rejoicing, as he explains in the parable of the prodigal son. The son had squandered his inheritance and had lived loosely with women, but he returned to his father to tell him he was sorry for what he had done. His father ran out to meet him, embraced him and kissed him, gave him the best robe, put shoes on his feet and a ring on his hand, and celebrated his return with a banquet of a fattened calf (cf. *Luke* 15:11-24). This is an image of God the Father welcoming back the sinner, no matter how many or how serious the sins he has committed.

We see this too in the prophecy of Ezekiel:

> Again, when a wicked man turns away from the wickedness he has committed and does what is lawful and right, he shall save his life. Because he considered and turned away from all the transgressions which he had committed, he shall surely live, he shall not die… Therefore I will judge you, O house of Israel, every one according to his ways, says the Lord God. Repent and turn from all your transgressions, lest iniquity be your ruin. Cast away from you all the transgressions which you have committed against me, and get yourselves a new heart and a new spirit: Why will you die, O house of Israel? For I have no pleasure in the death of anyone, says the Lord God; so turn, and live (*Ezek* 18:26-28; 30-32).

So it is very clear that mortal sins of themselves will not send anyone to hell, as long as the sinner is truly sorry for them.

21 Who was Sr Josefa Menendez, who had revelations of hell?

I have been reading a very interesting book by Sr Josefa Menendez, a Spanish nun, who had special revelations from God about hell. Can you tell me something about her and whether her writings have been approved by the Church?

Sr Josefa and her writings have been approved by the Church and, what is more, her cause of beatification has been opened.

Sister Josefa was born in Madrid on 4 February 1890. She felt called by God to the religious life and, after many trials, in 1920, at the age of 29, she entered the French convent of Les Feuillants in Poitiers as a Coadjutrix Sister of the Society of the Sacred Heart. She died there less than four years later.

Sr Josefa carried out her tasks in the convent with great grace and humility. When over the course of the next four years she received many revelations from God, she was moved to a deep sense of littleness and unworthiness. Her superiors had rarely seen anyone more obedient and docile, ever ready to submit to their authority and to sacrifice herself to do what was asked.

Sr Josefa was mentally sound and strong, very simple in her life of piety. The special graces and gifts she received from God, whose weight was often crushing, purified her. Some of the extraordinary visions and revelations shook her to the core and at times required an almost superhuman endurance. Her superiors were convinced that they were truly from God.

Among her trials were temptations from the devil to doubt God's voice and her own religious vocation, but she remained strong and resisted the temptations. At times the devil tried to deceive her by appearing as Our Lord or Our Lady and, when that failed, he attacked her with grievous bodily pains. These included beating her with an invisible fist, especially during her prayer, and violently dragging her away from the chapel or preventing her from entering it. Even while in the presence of other nuns, her clothes were set on fire and she suffered burns that took a long time to heal. At times the devil appeared to her in the form of a savage dog, a snake, or a human being.

Among her other sufferings were being taken to hell numerous times, where she spent long hours in unspeakable agony, suffering bodily pains and hearing the cries of hatred, despair and pain of the damned. After those experiences she looked on suffering, no matter how severe, as very little to bear, if by it she could save a soul from hell. As if this weren't enough, she also had visions of the passion and death of Our Lord, suffering in her body the same pains that Christ did. In spite of all this she humbly went about her normal daily routine in the convent.

Because of her simplicity, Our Lord once told her: "I will reveal to you the burning secrets of my Heart and many souls will profit by them. I want you to write down and keep all I tell you. It will be read when you are in heaven. Do not think that I make use of you because of your merits, but I want souls to realise how my power makes use of poor and miserable instruments." On 7 June 1923, Our Lord said: "If I could have found a more wretched creature, I should have chosen her for my special love, and through her revealed the longings of my Heart. But I have not found one, and so I have chosen you."

Under obedience, Sr Josefa wrote down her revelations, day by day. They were published in 1938 in Toulouse under the title *Un Appel à l'Amour* by the Apostleship of Prayer. Cardinal Eugenio Pacelli, later to become Pope Pius XII, wrote a foreword for the book. A second, more complete edition was published in French in 1944 with the *Imprimatur* of Archbishop Saliège of Toulouse. It was translated into English as *The Way of Divine Love*. The authenticity of her account is attested to by her superior and her spiritual director, Father Boyer, O.P.

Sr Josefa died on 29 December 1923 at the age of thirty-three. *The Way of Divine Love*, published in Milwaukee in 1972, bears the *Nihil Obstat* and *Imprimatur* of that Archdiocese. There are recent editions of the book published by TAN and Baronius.

22 What were some of Sr Josefa Menendez's revelations?

Can you tell me some of Sr Josefa Menendez's revelations, including some about hell? I find this topic very interesting.

Sr Josefa, as we recall, spent just four years in a convent in Poitiers, France, before her death in 1923 at the age of thirty-three. She was a privileged soul, on whom Our Lord poured out many graces, at the same time as he gave her an extraordinary share in his sufferings. It was during those years in the convent that Sr Josefa received numerous revelations from Our Lord and Our Lady. She wrote them down, as Our Lord asked her to do, so that they could benefit many people after her death.

One of the most frequent themes of the messages was Jesus' overwhelming love for mankind through his Sacred Heart. It was as if he were repeating in the twentieth century what he had made so clear to St Margaret Mary Alacoque in the seventeenth. At the same time it was a preparation for the revelation of the Divine Mercy that Christ would give to St Faustina Kowalska a few years later, beginning in 1931. On the night of 24 February 1921 Our Lord called Sr Josefa to spread this devotion: "The world does not know the mercy of my Heart. I intend to enlighten them through you.... I want you to be the apostle of my love and mercy."

Our Lord revealed his great compassion and love for sinners, telling Sr Josefa: "Do you not know that the more wretched a soul is, the more I love her? ... The fact that I have chosen a soul does not mean that her faults and miseries are wiped out. But if in all humility that soul acknowledges her failings and atones by little acts of generosity and love, above all, if she trusts me, if she throws herself into my Heart, she gives me more glory and does more good to souls than if she had not fallen. What does her wretchedness matter to me, if she gives me the love that I want?" (20 October 1922) And on the feast of the Sacred Heart, 8 June 1923, Jesus told her: "I will love you, and by the love I have for you souls will realise how much I love them. Since I forgive you so often, they will recognise my mercy."

On one occasion Our Lord told Sr Josefa what he was thinking when he washed the feet of the apostles in the Last Supper:

> In the first place I would teach souls how pure they must be to receive me in Holy Communion. I also wished to remind those who would have the misfortune to sin that they can always recover their innocence through the sacrament of Penance. And I washed the feet of my apostles with my own hands, so that those who have consecrated themselves to apostolic work may follow my example, and treat sinners with humility and gentleness, as also all others that are entrusted to their care. I

girded myself with a white linen cloth to remind them that apostles need to be girded with abnegation and mortification, if they hope to exert any real influence on souls. I wished also to teach them mutual charity, which is ever ready to excuse the faults of others, to conceal them and extenuate them, and never to reveal them. Lastly, the water poured on the feet of my apostles denotes the zeal that burned in my Heart for the salvation of the world (25 February 1923).

Some of the most striking revelations of the importance of love come in Sr Josefa's numerous visions of hell. She writes: "One of these damned souls cried out: 'This is my torture... that I want to love and cannot; there is nothing left me but hatred and despair. If one of us could so much as make a single act of love... This would no longer be hell... but we cannot, we live on hatred and malevolence.'" Another soul cried out: "The greatest of our torments here is that we are not able to love him. While we hunger for love, we are consumed with desire of it, but it is too late" (23 March 1922). This is combined with Our Lord's burning desire to save souls from going to hell. On one occasion he told Sr Josefa: "Help me; help me to make my love for men known, for I come to tell them that in vain will they seek happiness apart from me, for they will not find it. Suffer, Josefa, and love, for we two must win these souls" (13 June 1923).

23 Is it true that Pope Francis once denied the existence of hell?

I understand Pope Francis has been quoted as saying that hell doesn't exist and that the souls of those who reject God at the end simply disappear. Did the Pope really say that?

Pope Francis most certainly did not say that. Like all faithful Catholics, he believed in hell and he spoke of it on several occasions during his years as Pope. The source of the misleading statement was Eugenio Scalfari, a 93-year-old retired journalist, former editor of *La Repubblica* and avowed atheist, who has become a good friend of the Pope. After a recent meeting with the Holy Father, Scalfari wrote on 28 March 2018 that the Pope told him, "Hell does not exist" and that the souls of those who reject God at the end of their life simply cease to exist.

According to Vatican spokesman Greg Burke, Pope Francis invited Scalfari to have a "private meeting for the occasion of Easter" and the meeting was not a formal interview. In his earlier interviews with the Pope in 2013 and 2015, Scalfari took no notes and did not record the conversation, limiting himself to reconstructing the conversation later on the basis of his own memory, and that was obviously the case this time as well.

The reality is that Pope Francis spoke several times about the existence of hell. In a warning to the Mafia in 2014, he said: "Convert! There is still time, so that you don't end up in hell. That is what awaits you if you continue on this path. You had a father and a mother: think of them. Cry a little and convert."

Then in his 2016 Message for Lent he wrote: "The danger always remains that by a constant refusal to open the doors of their hearts to Christ who knocks on them in the poor, the proud, rich and powerful will end up condemning themselves and plunging into the eternal abyss of solitude which is hell."

Fr John Wauck, a lecturer at the Pontifical University of the Holy Cross in Rome, commented on the Scalfari statement in a radio interview on "The *Crux* of the matter": "My first reaction, especially because this wasn't the first time, was, 'There goes crazy Scalfari again.' He's getting a headline out of something outrageous that seems to be in complete contradiction to the Christian faith and other things Francis has said."

Rather than being scandalised, Wauck saw it as an opportunity to explain what the Church teaches on hell. He said: "Hell is actually God's way of taking us seriously. If we're able to determine our eternity in a good sense, meaning eternal life, God, happiness, delight, all of which will last forever on the basis of what we've done, it makes sense there's a flip side. Sometimes we think hell seems kind of disproportionate, but heaven's also disproportionate.

God has skin in the game ... he's given us everything, and hell is a reminder of what we can turn our back on, which is something infinite."

24 Did Christ really descend into hell?

After we had finished saying the Apostles Creed recently my daughter asked me why Jesus descended into hell after his death on the Cross. I hadn't thought about the question before and was unsure of the answer. Can you help me?

First of all, let me say that Jesus did not descend to the hell of the damned, but rather to the place or state where all those who had died before him and who deserved to go to heaven were awaiting his death and resurrection. This place is sometimes referred to as the "Limbo of the Fathers." It was not a place of suffering but rather of great happiness, in the expectation of a final reward in heaven.

Christ went there following his death to announce to the souls waiting there the good news of their redemption. As the Catechism puts it, "In his human soul united to his divine person, the dead Christ went down to the realm of the dead. He opened heaven's gates for the just who had gone before him." (*CCC* 637) It also says: "Jesus did not descend into hell to deliver the damned, nor to destroy the hell of damnation, but to free the just who had gone before him." (*CCC* 633)

The confusion arises in the English translation of the Hebrew word *Sheol* or the Greek word *Hades*, rendered in Latin as *Inferus*. These words could be translated as the "underworld", the "lower regions" or the "realm of the dead". In the understanding of the people at that time, it was the abode of the dead, of all those who had died, and was not specifically the place of eternal punishment that today we call hell. St Paul refers to it, writing to the Ephesians: "When it says 'he ascended', what can it mean if not that he descended right down to the lower regions of the earth? The one who rose higher than all the heavens to fill all things is none other than the one who descended" (*Eph* 4:9-10).

A new version of the Apostles Creed avoids this difficulty by saying that Christ "descended to the dead", a much better translation.

Purgatory

25 What is purgatory and why should it exist?

I have never really understood the Church's teaching on purgatory. If we have been baptised and have tried to lead a good life, and we have repented of all our serious sins, why doesn't God take us straight to heaven when we die?

As its name suggests, purgatory is a state of purging, purgation, of the soul of the effects of sin after death so that it is pure and able to go to heaven. The *Catechism of the Catholic Church* teaches: "All who die in God's grace and friendship, but still imperfectly purified, are indeed assured of their eternal salvation; but after death they undergo purification, so as to achieve the holiness necessary to enter the joy of heaven" (*CCC* 1030).

The words "imperfectly purified" imply that the soul must be perfectly pure in order to go to heaven. We see this in the Scriptures, for example in the Letter to the Hebrews: "Strive for peace with all men, and for the holiness without which no one will see the Lord" (*Heb* 12:14). This is understandable. In order to go to heaven and see God face to face, where all is holiness, light, purity, the soul must be all holy, all pure, without any stain of sin.

The person has died "in God's grace and friendship", that is, with sorrow for their sins and love for God. In Catholic terminology, they are in the state of grace, not in that of mortal sin, so that they are assured of going to heaven, but their soul is not yet perfectly purified from the effects of sin. This purification takes place after death in the state we call purgatory.

The traditional teaching of the Church is that the soul must be purified of three realities: temporal punishment owing for sin, attachments or bad habits caused by sin, and any lack of sorrow for venial sins.

As for temporal punishment, every sin we commit, whether

venial or mortal, requires that we do something to make up for it. This punishment, by the way, is called temporal, from the Latin word for time, because it must be made up in time. That time can be either here on earth, or after death in the time we might spend in purgatory.

The understanding is that, in addition to asking God to forgive our sins, we must do something to make up for the harm caused to God and the Church by our sins. That is, sin leaves a certain debt to be paid to God's justice and holiness before the soul is perfectly purified and ready for heaven. In his mercy, God does not ask that we make up wholly for the harm our sins have caused to his infinite majesty and love, for we could never do that. But we must do something. This is understandable. If we damage the property of another and ask to be forgiven, the owner may forgive us, but he will still want us to pay for the damage we have caused.

God does the same. That is why, for example, the Church gives us days and seasons of penance in the Church calendar, where we strive to do more penance to make up for some of the temporal punishment owing for our sins. Really, all our good deeds done in the state of grace help to whittle away our debt: our prayers, work, penances, acts of charity to others, etc.

And, of course, so do indulgences. Indulgences are the remission before God of part or all of the temporal punishment owing for our sins through doing acts prescribed by the Church, such as saying certain prayers, making the Way of the Cross, etc. In order to gain an indulgence, we must be in the state of grace, and we must have the intention of gaining the indulgence. To gain the remission of all the temporal punishment through what is called a plenary indulgence, we must do the prescribed act, reject all attachment to sin, even venial sin, and also pray for the intentions of the Pope, go to confession within a few weeks and receive Holy Communion.

Here is where what I like to call our "spiritual bank account" comes in. We all have a spiritual bank account. When we are baptised, our account is opened with a large positive balance. The soul has been freed from all sin, original sin and personal sins in the case of an adult; it is filled with sanctifying grace, which is a sharing in the life of God and makes us holy and pleasing to God; the Blessed Trinity comes to abide in the soul, and we are made children of God.

Over time we increase the balance by our good deeds, prayers, penances, the reception of the sacraments, etc. And we withdraw from it through our sins and other misdeeds. If we commit a mortal, or serious, sin, we lose the state of grace altogether and we are in the state of mortal sin, making our balance negative. At any one time, our balance will be positive or negative. If when we die it is negative, because we haven't sufficiently made up for our sins, we will go to purgatory. And of course, if we die in the state of unrepented mortal sin, we will go to hell.

To avoid purgatory, our balance must be positive when we die. For this reason, we should try to commit fewer sins and do all we can to make up for our sins, so that our balance is positive. Since we can never know what our balance is at any one time, we do well to assume that it is negative and strive to commit fewer sins and increase our good deeds and penances. Naturally, God in his infinite mercy may very well overlook a negative balance and take us straight to heaven. But we should not take that for granted.

St Catherine of Genoa (1447-1510) puts it like this:

> No one is barred from heaven. Whoever wants to enter heaven may do so because God is all-merciful. Our Lord will welcome us into glory with his arms wide open. The Almighty is so pure, however, that if a person is conscious of the least trace of imperfection and at the same time understands that purgatory is ordained to do away with such impediments, the soul enters this place of purification glad to accept so great a mercy of God. The worst suffering of these suffering souls is to have sinned against divine Goodness and not to have been purified in this life (*Treatise on Purgatory*, 12).

The second reality of which we must be purified is any bad habits or attachments caused by sin. This refers to serious bad habits and attachments. For example, we may be excessively attached to material possessions, to food and drink, to social media or other internet sites, to our good reputation, to gambling, etc. To go to heaven, we must be able to tell God that we love him with our whole heart, soul, mind and strength, and this is incompatible with any undue love for, any disordered attachment to, something here below.

And thirdly, we must be sorry for all our sins, including venial sins. If we are not sorry for a venial sin we will not go to hell, but we are not ready for heaven either. Loving God with our whole heart means we must be sorry for all our offences against him, including venial sins. If we are not sorry, we clearly do not love him.

If we strive to love God with our whole heart and to make up for our sins, if we truly strive for holiness, we have every chance of going straight to heaven, bypassing purgatory, when we die. But if we fall short, we should never forget that purgatory, while a state of suffering, is the happiest place outside of heaven.

26 Is there any evidence for purgatory in the Bible?

I have many Protestant friends and when we discuss my belief in purgatory they always tell me there is nothing about it in the Bible and therefore we shouldn't believe in it. Are there any scriptural texts I can use to show them that purgatory is a reality?

Before looking at the biblical texts, there is abundant evidence in the first centuries of the Church's belief in a state of purification after death, or purgatory. One of the Fathers of the Church goes so far as to say that the custom was so widespread that it was believed to have been taught by the very apostles. This evidence from tradition, even if there were nothing in the Bible, should be enough to convince a well-meaning person of the advisability of praying for those who have died, and therefore of the reality of purgatory.

As regards scriptural texts, there are a number which are frequently used to back up the Church's teaching on purgatory, even if by themselves they do not "prove" its existence.

Perhaps the most convincing one is from the Second Book of the Maccabees in the Old Testament. After a battle in which a number of Jewish soldiers have been killed, it is discovered that under the tunic of each of the fallen is a token of the idols of Jamnia. To wear such a token is of course sinful. The account tells us that "they turned to prayer, begging that the sin which had been committed might be wholly blotted out" (*2 Mac* 12:42). Judas, their leader, then took up a collection to be sent to Jerusalem for a sin offering on behalf of the fallen. "In doing this he acted very well and honourably, taking account of the resurrection. For if he were not expecting that those who had fallen would rise again, it would have been superfluous and foolish to pray for the dead. But if he was looking to the splendid reward that is laid up for those who fall asleep in godliness, it was a holy and pious thought. Therefore, he made atonement for the dead, that they might be delivered from their sin" (*2 Mac* 12:43-45). This passage clearly shows the belief of the Jews in the second century before Christ that sins could be atoned for after death, implying the belief in purgatory.

This belief carried over to the first Christians, who continued the practice of praying for the dead. Because the belief and custom were so deeply ingrained and generally accepted, there was no need to mention them explicitly in the New Testament. Nonetheless, there are some passages which can be understood as referring to purification of sins after death.

The book of Revelation, for example, says that "nothing unclean shall enter" the heavenly Jerusalem (*Rev* 21:27). A similar text is found in the Letter to the Hebrews, which reads: "Strive for peace with all men, and for the holiness without which no one will see the Lord" (*Heb* 12:14). Both of these texts are telling us that in order to enter heaven, where all is light, purity, holiness, love, the soul must be perfectly pure, without any stain of sin. This is understandable in human terms. If we were invited to a dinner or reception with an important person, we would put on our best clothes and make sure they were spotlessly clean. How much more important it is, then, for the soul to be without any stain of sin in order to enter into the presence of the all-holy God in heaven.

Then too, Jesus himself says in the Sermon on the Mount, with regard to someone in debt to another: "Make friends quickly with your accuser, while you are going with him to court, lest your accuser hand you over to the judge, and the judge to the guard, and you be put in prison; truly, I say to you, you will never get out till you have paid the last penny" (*Matt* 5:25-26). While in itself this text cannot prove anything regarding purgatory, it has been used to speak about a debt before God owing for sin, which must be paid in full before the soul is free. In the second century, Tertullian, for example, understands by prison the realm of the dead, and by the last penny the sins that must expiated there before the person is free to go to heaven (cf. *De anima* 58).

Another text which is often used comes in the First Letter to the Corinthians. Here St Paul is speaking of how each person builds his life on the foundation of Jesus Christ, and in the judgment the quality of his work will be "revealed with fire, and the fire will test what sort of work each one has done. If the work which any man has built on the foundation survives, he will receive a reward. If any man's work is burned up, he will suffer loss, though he himself will be saved, but only as through fire" (*1 Cor* 3:13-15). The Latin Fathers of the Church understood this passage as referring to a transient purifying punishment by fire in the next life, and hence to purgatory (cf. St Augustine, *Enarr. in Ps.* 37, 3; St Caesarius of Arles, *Sermo* 179).

While none of these passages can be taken to "prove" the existence of purgatory to the satisfaction of a non-believer, they do make a powerful case for it in light of the Church's constant practice of praying for the dead.

27 Did they believe in purgatory in the early Church?

I was talking recently with a Protestant friend about praying for a mutual acquaintance who had passed away and she denied there was any need for it since there is no purgatory and the soul would be already in heaven. Is there any evidence in the early Church of prayer for the faithful departed?

The tradition in the early Church of praying for those who have died so that they may be purified of their sins is overwhelming. The custom is set in stone on the tombs of Christians of the first centuries, where we find inscriptions like: "Eternal light shine upon thee, Timothea, in Christ"; "Let [the reader] pray to God to take to himself her spirit holy and pure" and "Thee, O heavenly Father, we implore to have mercy." If the early Christians thought everyone who had died went straight to heaven, they would not have prayed for them.

Around the year 216 Tertullian describes how the Church prayed for the dead and offered Mass for them on the anniversary of their death: "A woman, after the death of her husband ... prays for his soul and asks that he may, while waiting, find rest; and that he may share in the first resurrection. And each year, on the anniversary of his death, she offers the sacrifice" (*Monogamy* 10:1–2). The sacrifice is, of course, the celebration of the Mass.

In the middle of the fourth century, St Cyril of Jerusalem writes of the Mass: "Then we make mention ... of all among us who have already fallen asleep, for we believe that it will be of very great benefit to the souls of those for whom the petition is carried up, while this holy and most solemn sacrifice is laid out" (*Catechetical Lectures* 23:5:9).

Around the year 392 St John Chrysostom writes of the holy souls: "Let us help and commemorate them. If Job's sons were purified by their father's sacrifice (cf. *Job* 1:5), why would we doubt that our offerings for the dead bring them some consolation? Let us not hesitate to help those who have died and to offer our prayers for them" (*Homilies on First Corinthians* 41:5).

Then too, well known is St Monica's request to her son Augustine just before her death: "Lay this body anywhere...This only I ask of you, that you remember me at the altar of the Lord, wherever you may be" (St Augustine, *Confessions* 9, 10-11).

St Augustine himself around the year 421 writes: "That there should be some fire even after this life is not incredible, and it can be inquired into and either be discovered or left hidden whether some of the faithful may be saved, some more slowly and some more quickly in the greater or lesser degree in which they loved the good things that perish, through a certain purgatorial fire" (*Handbook on Faith, Hope, and Charity* 18:69).

St Caesarius of Arles, who died in 452, said in a sermon: "If we neither give thanks to God in tribulations nor redeem our own sins by good works, we shall have to remain in that purgatorial fire as long as it takes the aforesaid lesser sins to be consumed" (*Sermon 179*, 2).

So widespread was the custom in the early Church of praying and offering Masses for the faithful departed that St Isidore of Seville could write in the seventh century: "To offer the sacrifice for the repose of the faithful departed is a custom observed all over the world. For this reason we believe that it is a custom taught by the very apostles" (*On ecclesiastical offices*, 1).

These texts are just a handful of the many that could be cited from the early Church. It is clear from them that the custom of praying and offering Masses for the dead, based on the corresponding belief in purgatory, was universally accepted and practised from the very beginning. Even if there were nothing at all in the Bible about it, we would still believe in it as coming from the life and practice of the Church. The practice was not challenged until the sixteenth century, when Protestants denied it.

The *Catechism of the Catholic Church* sums it up: "From the beginning the Church has honoured the memory of the dead and offered prayers in suffrage for them, above all the Eucharistic sacrifice, so that, thus purified, they may attain the beatific vision of God. The Church also commends almsgiving, indulgences and works of penance undertaken on behalf of the dead" (*CCC* 1032).

So, belief in purgatory rests on a very solid foundation indeed. It would be foolish and dangerous to deny it. Really, to be pitied are those who deny the existence of purgatory and who may one day end up there with no one to pray for them because they fostered the belief that it doesn't exist.

28 Apparitions of souls in purgatory

I know that the Church has always believed in purgatory, but is there any evidence apart from Scripture and tradition that it actually exists? My Protestant friends think we are wrong on this.

As we have seen, the scriptural evidence for belief in a state of purification after death is strong, and the evidence from the Church's tradition over the centuries of praying and offering Masses for the faithful departed is overwhelming.

If someone still remains sceptical, and of course many do, perhaps the numerous apparitions of souls from purgatory can help them. There are a good number of books with accounts of these apparitions and, frankly, they are very convincing. Let me relate just a few accounts, some of them taken from the book *Hungry Souls* by Dutch psychologist Gerard van den Aardweg (TAN Books, Charlotte, North Carolina, 2012). Another recent book of apparitions is *Visions of Purgatory – A Private Revelation* (Scepter 2014). It gives the accounts of numerous souls appearing to a monk in the second half of the twentieth century.

Van den Aardweg describes visiting a modest museum in the church of the Sacred Heart of Suffrage very near the Vatican in Rome. The museum was started in 1893 by Fr Victor Jouët, founder of the Archconfraternity of the Sacred Heart of Jesus for Aid to the Holy Souls. At present the museum contains ten items, most of them consisting of burn marks of hands and fingers left by souls from purgatory on books or clothing.

One of the most impressive is the nightshirt of Joseph Leleux. On eleven consecutive nights in 1789 Leleux heard frightening noises in his house in Wodecq, Belgium. Then on 21 June his mother, who had died twenty-seven years before, appeared to him and reminded him that he had an obligation to have Masses celebrated for her soul. She reproached him for his wayward life and begged him to change his ways and work for the Church. Then she laid her hand on the sleeve of his nightshirt, burning into it a clearly marked imprint of her hand. Leleux converted and founded a congregation of pious lay people. He died with a reputation for holiness in 1825.

Another item is from Father Panzini, a former abbot from Mantua, Italy, who appeared to the Venerable Isabella Fornari, abbess of the Poor Clares in Todi on the eve of All Souls Day in 1731. He left an imprint of his left hand and a cross burned deeply into the wood of Mother Isabella's work table, another of his hand on a sheet of paper and a third on the sleeve of her tunic. The latter burn passed through the tunic and burned her shirt, leaving a blood stain on it.

Yet another impressive burn mark from a soul in purgatory is kept at the shrine of Our Lady of Czestochowa in Poland, in the care of the Order of St Paul the First Hermit. According to an account written around 1890, two of the priests at the shrine had promised one another that the one who died first would give the other a sign from the next life. When considerable time had passed after the death of one of them, the other was wondering what had happened. Then when he was folding the linen corporal at the end of Mass a hand suddenly appeared, laid itself on the corporal and disappeared. It left a clearly-defined burn that passed through many layers of the folded corporal.

The reason for the burn marks is that the souls in purgatory are frequently seen in their apparitions as if on fire. St Margaret Mary Alacoque, who did much to promote devotion to the Sacred Heart, relates the following experience: "When I was praying before the Blessed Sacrament on the feast of Corpus Christi, a person enveloped in fire suddenly stood before me. From the pitiable state the soul was in, I knew it was in purgatory and I wept bitterly. This soul told me it was that of a Benedictine, who had once heard my confession and ordered me to go to Holy Communion. As a reward for this, God permitted him to ask me to help him in his sufferings. He asked me to apply to him all I should do or suffer for a period of three months... It would be difficult for me to describe what I had to endure during those three months. He never left me and seeing him, as it were, on fire and in such terrible pain, I could do nothing but groan and weep almost incessantly..." After three months of her hard penances, the soul went to heaven.

In modern times both St Padre Pio and St Faustina had visits from souls in purgatory. In short, purgatory is real. And it is for all, not just Catholics. It would be very foolish not to believe in it.

29 What sort of suffering do souls have in purgatory?

What do we know about the suffering of souls in purgatory?

The souls in purgatory suffer two principal pains: the pain of loss, of being deprived of the sight of God, and the pain of sense, likened to fire. All agree that the greatest of these pains is that of loss. We can understand this in terms of human love. When someone loves another intensely and cannot be with their beloved, they suffer greatly. In purgatory, as the soul's disordered love for the world and for itself is gradually purged, their love for God grows proportionately, and at the end it is so great that the suffering of not being with God is exceedingly intense.

There is also the pain of sense, which is likened to fire. In the numerous apparitions of souls in purgatory appearing to people on earth, many of them appear to be on fire, and the heat is often experienced by the person to whom they appear. Even though the pain of fire is intense and difficult to bear, the pain of loss, of being deprived of the sight of God, is even greater.

It is a common teaching, too, that the slightest pain of purgatory is greater than the greatest pain one can suffer on earth. St Thomas Aquinas deals with this in the Supplement of his *Summa Theologiae*. He explains:

> In purgatory there will be a twofold pain; one will be the pain of loss, namely the delay of the divine vision, and the pain of sense, namely punishment by corporeal fire. With regard to both, the least pain of purgatory surpasses the greatest pain of this life.
>
> For the more a thing is desired the more painful is its absence. And since after this life the holy souls desire the Sovereign Good with the most intense longing, – both because their longing is not held back by the weight of the body, and because, had there been no obstacle, they would already have gained the goal of enjoying the Sovereign Good, – it follows that they grieve exceedingly for their delay.
>
> Again, since pain is not hurt, but the sense of hurt, the

> more sensitive a thing is, the greater the pain caused by that which hurts it: wherefore hurts inflicted on the more sensible parts cause the greatest pain. And because all bodily sensation is from the soul, it follows of necessity that the soul feels the greatest pain when a hurt is inflicted on the soul itself. That the soul suffers pain from the bodily fire is at present taken for granted, for we shall treat of this matter further on (cf. Suppl., q. 70, art. 3). Therefore, it follows that the pain of purgatory, both of loss and of sense, surpasses all the pains of this life (Suppl., Appendix 1, q. 2, art. 1).

Even though the pain of purgatory is so great, the souls there welcome their suffering, because it purifies them for their entry into heaven, of which they are assured. Here on earth we can never be absolutely sure that we will go to heaven when we die, even though we may regard it as very likely. The souls in purgatory are absolutely sure of heaven, and so they are very happy, happier than we are on earth.

Their great suffering and at the same time their great happiness are mutually compatible. It is like a person who has just emerged from surgery, wracked with pain but with the joy of knowing they will now recover their health. Confirmation of the great joy experienced by the souls in purgatory comes from an elderly nun, who while in purgatory appeared to a monk and said: "The greatest happiness for a soul is to be in heaven. It is eternal bliss. But immediately after this, there is no joy greater than to savour the joys of purgatory" (*Visions of Purgatory*, Scepter 2014, p. 154). This nun was in purgatory herself. She would know.

Not for nothing does the Church refer to the "blessed souls" in purgatory. Pope Benedict XVI speaks of their suffering as arising from the encounter of the soul with the love of Christ. In his encyclical *Spe salvi*, on hope, he writes: "This encounter with [Christ], as it burns us, transforms and frees us, allowing us to become truly ourselves... His gaze, the touch of his heart heals us through an undeniably painful transformation 'as through fire'. But it is a blessed pain, in which the holy power of his love sears through us like a flame, enabling us to become totally ourselves and thus totally of God... The pain of love becomes our salvation and our joy" (n. 47).

30 Are there different degrees of suffering in purgatory?

I was wondering whether the souls in purgatory might experience different degrees of suffering from one another, and whether their suffering might gradually become less over time. Do we know anything about this?

As is to be expected, the Church has never defined anything about the possible degrees of suffering or whether the suffering might decrease over time. But from the numerous accounts of apparitions of souls in purgatory to people on earth we can glean some information. It should always be remembered, however, that these accounts form part of what we call private revelation, and they need not be believed.

What follows answers your questions. It is taken from *An unpublished manuscript on purgatory*, a fascinating account of messages from Sr Mary Gabriel, a French nun in purgatory, to Sr Mary of the Cross, another nun from her convent in the nineteenth century. Sr Mary Gabriel died in 1871 and began communicating in 1874. Her last message from purgatory was in 1887, and in 1890 she spoke from heaven. The document was published in English in 1968 with the *Imprimatur* of the archbishop of Baltimore, and by 1975 it had gone through eight printings totalling 28,000 copies. The introduction to the book explains that the spiritual director of Sr Mary of the Cross and several theologians were firmly convinced that the messages were authentic and that they contained nothing contrary to the faith.

So, are there different degrees of suffering in purgatory and do they lessen over time? The nun in purgatory says yes. She refers to stages: "I can tell you about the different degrees of purgatory because I have passed through them. In the great purgatory there are several stages. In the lowest and most painful, like a temporary hell, are the sinners who have committed terrible crimes during life and whose death surprised them in that state. It was almost a miracle that they were saved, and often by the prayers of holy parents or other pious persons. Sometimes they did not even have time to confess their sins and the world thought them lost, but God, whose mercy is infinite, gave them at the moment of death the contrition necessary for their salvation on account of one or more good actions which they performed during life. For such souls, purgatory is terrible. It is a real hell with this difference, that in hell they curse God, whereas we bless him and thank him for having saved us.

"Next to these come the souls, who though they did not commit great crimes like the others, were indifferent to God. They did not fulfill their Easter duties and were also converted at the point of death. Perhaps they were unable to receive Holy Communion. They are in purgatory for the long years of indifference. They suffer unheard of pains and are abandoned either without prayers or if they are said for them, they are not allowed to profit by them. There are in this stage of purgatory religious of both sexes, who were tepid, neglectful of their duties, indifferent towards Jesus, also priests who did not exercise their sacred ministry with the reverence due to the Sovereign Majesty and who did not instill the love of God sufficiently into the souls confided to their care. I was in this stage of purgatory.

"In the second purgatory are the souls of those who died with venial sins not fully expiated before death, or with mortal sins that have been forgiven but for which they have not made entire satisfaction to the Divine Justice. In this part of purgatory, there are also different degrees according to the merits of each soul. Thus the purgatory of the consecrated souls or of those who have received more abundant graces, is longer and far more painful than that of ordinary people of the world.

"Lastly, there is the purgatory of desire which is called the *Threshold*. Very few escape this. To avoid it altogether, one must ardently desire heaven and the vision of God. That is rare, rarer than people think, because even pious people are afraid of God and have not, therefore, a sufficiently strong desire of going to heaven. This purgatory has its very painful martyrdom like the others. The deprivation of the sight of our loving Jesus adds to the intense suffering." Elsewhere she says that, although the suffering in this stage is intense, there is no fire there.

She also says that in the second stage she saw the Blessed Virgin for the first time. "In the first stage, we never saw her. The sight of her encourages us and this beloved Mother speaks to us of heaven. While we see her, our sufferings are greatly diminished." In 1878 she said: "I am much relieved as I am no longer in the fire. I have now only the insatiable desire to see God, a suffering cruel enough indeed, but I feel that the end of my exile is at hand and that I am soon to leave this place where I long for God with all my heart."

31 Is there time in purgatory?

I have always wondered whether there is time as we know it in purgatory. Has the Church said anything about this?

There has to be some sort of time in purgatory because souls are not there forever, as they are in heaven and hell. The numerous souls in purgatory who have appeared to people on earth bear this out, since they sometimes say how long they have been in purgatory. But exactly how this time is experienced in purgatory itself we cannot really know until we get there.

Referring to the fire which burns away the effects of sin in purgatory, Pope Benedict XVI says in his encyclical *Spe salvi* (2007): "It is clear that we cannot calculate the 'duration' of this transforming burning in terms of the chronological measurements of this world. The transforming 'moment' of this encounter eludes earthly time-reckoning – it is the heart's time, it is the time of 'passage' to communion with God in the Body of Christ" (n. 47).

As is to be expected, the Church has never pronounced on the question of for how long souls are in purgatory or on how they experience time there. There are numerous accounts of souls in purgatory appearing on earth which shed light on this, but since they are private revelations, we are not required to believe them. Nonetheless, they can be helpful in answering your question.

One helpful account is that of a man who died in France in July, 1870, and appeared numerous times to his daughter, a nun in

Belgium. The man told his daughter in October: "If I shall have to remain in purgatory three months more it will seem an eternity." From this it seems that he had some idea of the passage of months, since he had been in purgatory for three months when he made the statement. On November 30 he said: "It seems an eternity to me since I arrived in purgatory. At present my greatest torment is the intense longing to behold God and to enjoy his possession." Here he expresses the idea that even a short time can seem like an eternity when there is an intense longing to be with God.

As regards for how long, measured by earth time, souls are in purgatory, this same account mentions several cases. The man himself, who had died "like a saint" in the judgment of his children, was in purgatory from July 17 until Christmas Eve that same year, a relatively short time. He told another nun in the convent that her father, who had neglected his religious duties for a long time and had died without the sacraments, would be in purgatory for 20 years. He also told her that her sister, who had died 16 years before at the age of eight, had been released from purgatory a short time before and was now in heaven.

In the account we have just seen in *An unpublished manuscript on purgatory*, the nun in purgatory said that thousands of souls enter purgatory each day and that "most of them remain 30 to 40 years, some for longer periods, others for shorter. I tell you this in terms of earthly calculations because here it is quite different… I have been here eight years and it seems to me like ten thousand."

An explanation of this unusual experience of time comes from another soul in purgatory, who commented in an apparition: "You cannot understand this, but here in purgatory the time and the intensity of one's pains form a single thing. Our greatest suffering is our nostalgia for God. The more we wait for someone we love, the more slowly the time passes, and the greater is our suffering in this waiting" (*Visions of Purgatory*, p. 152).

People often ask about Our Lady's statement at Fatima that a 12-year-old local girl would be in purgatory until the end of the world. It is difficult to explain how this could be, if indeed Our Lady was reported accurately. It could very well be, however, that the girl would have been there for a very long time if no one prayed for her, but with the many people who have prayed for her since then, her time was considerably shortened.

32 Is purgatory somehow a manifestation of God's mercy?

Our priest recently said that we should see purgatory as a manifestation of God's mercy. I don't understand how so much suffering after death can be a manifestation of mercy. Can you help me?

I agree completely with your priest. Really, all God's actions are manifestations of his infinite mercy, including giving us purgatory, where we can make up for our sins after death. Personally, I like to explain purgatory in terms of three divine attributes: his holiness, his justice and his mercy.

God's holiness demands that in order to enter heaven, where all is light, beauty, love, purity – holiness, in a word – the soul must be completely pure, free from every stain of sin, from all temporal punishment owing for sin, from all bad habits or attachments caused by sin, from all lack of sorrow for venial sins. In a word, it must be clothed in the wedding garment of holiness.

We can understand this in human terms. For example, if we were invited to a reception at the house of our governor, or to an audience with the Pope, it is understandable that we would not think of going there in old, dirty clothes, with our hair not properly combed, etc. All the more then, to go to heaven, where we are in the presence of the Blessed Trinity, Our Lady, the angels and saints, how pure the soul must be! The Letter to the Hebrews speaks of "that holiness without which no one will see the Lord" (*Heb* 12:14). So, God's holiness demands that our soul be all pure, all holy, in order to spend eternity with him. If when we die it is not perfectly purified, God in his holiness has given us purgatory so that we may become holy ourselves.

God's justice, or fairness, also seems to imply the need for purgatory. Imagine, for example, that two people have committed the same sins throughout their life, and one has tried to make up for them through a multitude of good works, prayers, penances, indulgences, etc., and the other has done nothing, or very little, to make up. It doesn't seem right, or fair, that when they die they should both go straight to heaven, where they will be completely happy. God is just, and if we have a debt of temporal punishment owing for our sins, in justice we must pay off the debt before we can spend eternity with him. What is more, our sins cause harm to the Mystical Body of the Church, as well as to God and ourselves, and we must make up for them before we are ready for heaven.

And, finally, God's mercy is manifested in purgatory too. First of all, in his mercy God does not ask us to make up completely for our sins. It would be impossible for us to do so, taking into account that we are only God's creatures and we have sinned against the infinite majesty of our Creator. Then too, in his mercy God has given us the Church to teach us how to live, so as to avoid sin and grow in virtue, he gives us the sacraments to strengthen us in grace and pick us up when we have fallen, indulgences to make up for our temporal punishment, etc.

And above all, in his mercy he has given us purgatory itself, so that if we have not adequately made up for our sins before dying, we have a second chance after death. If there were no purgatory and we died with stains of sin on our soul, God would have to tell us that we cannot enter heaven, because our soul is not all pure, all holy. He would have to usher us to a state of natural happiness where we would never see God directly, a state which has traditionally been called Limbo. But in his mercy, God gives us the opportunity to make up after death for what we should have done in life. That is mercy indeed.

33 Should we always pray for those who have died?

In recent years I have found increasingly in funeral Masses that the priest implies that the deceased person is already in heaven and we should all give thanks for their life. Nothing is said about praying for the person's soul, something I have always believed in. Is this good?

This is a frequently asked question. As you say – and I have had the same experience – in many funeral Masses nothing is said about praying for the deceased person. Often the Mass booklet itself can have the title, "Mass of thanksgiving for the life of ..." While we should certainly give thanks to God for the life of any deceased person, it should be clear that the funeral Mass, or Mass of Christian burial, is never a Mass of thanksgiving.

The theme of the Mass is indicated in the Collect, or Opening Prayer, said by the priest. In funeral Masses this is always a prayer asking God to bring the person to the joy of eternal life, not thanking him for the life of the person.

It is in the priest's homily where it is often said that we are here to give thanks for the person's life, and even that we rejoice that the person is already enjoying the eternal reward so richly deserved for their good life. This is equivalent to "canonising" the person; that is, declaring them to be included in the canon or list of the saints in heaven. But this is something only the Pope can do, and he does it only after a long and painstaking study of the person's life of heroic virtue, accompanied by the verification of a second miracle. In the case of Australia's St Mary MacKillop, over 100 years passed from her death in 1909 to her canonisation by Pope Benedict XVI in 2010.

Don't misunderstand me. There is nothing wrong with extolling the deceased person's virtues and good works in an appropriate way. Indeed, it is good for those attending the Mass to hear about these good works, so that they can be inspired to live a better life themselves. But it should never be suggested that the person is already in heaven, since we cannot be certain of this, and it would deprive the person of perhaps much needed prayers. It is very difficult to go straight to heaven when we die. Rather, it is very good that specific mention be made of the importance of praying for the person's soul and of having Masses offered for them, no matter how good the person was. If the person is in fact already in heaven, the prayers will not be wasted. They will be channelled by God to some other intention.

And in any case, the person praying is always sanctified by those prayers. Looking at it more personally, we would not want to find ourselves in purgatory one day and not have our loved ones pray for us because the priest in our funeral Mass assured them we were in heaven.

St Thomas More, in his brilliant work *The Supplication of Souls*, writes as if from a soul in purgatory to those on earth, beseeching them to pray for the holy souls. He reminds us how easy it is to forget to do this:

> For if your father, your mother, your child, your brother, your sister, your husband, your wife, or a complete stranger, for that matter, lay within your sight in fire somewhere and you had the means to help them, what heart could be so hard, what stomach so imperturbable, that it could restfully sit at supper or sleep in bed and let a person lie and burn? We therefore find very true that old proverb, 'Out of sight, out of mind' (Scepter, New York 2002, p. 182).

Indeed, because we cannot see the souls suffering in purgatory, including perhaps some of our loved ones, we forget all about them, or assume they are already in heaven. St Thomas goes on to say that if we do not pray for the holy souls, we may find that if we go to purgatory ourselves others on earth will not pray for us:

> And yet surely, to tell the truth, we cannot with good reason much grumble against you for this. For while we were with you out there, we, in our overindulgence in that wretched world, likewise forgot our good friends here. And therefore we cannot be too surprised if God in his justice allows us to be forgotten by you as others before were forgotten by us. But we beseech our Lord, for both our sakes, to give you the grace to rectify on your side that fault common to us both, lest when you come here later, God out of like justice should allow you to be forgotten by those that you leave there behind you, as you forget us that have come here before you" (*ibid.*).

In short, we do well always to pray very much for the souls of those who have died, no matter how good they were in life. Then we can be sure that there will be many people to pray for us when we die. Also, the very fact that we pray for them helps us to keep in mind the reality of purgatory, and so it moves us to do all in our power to avoid going to purgatory ourselves. For example, we will struggle harder to avoid the occasions of sin, to be generous in our penances and other good deeds in order to make up for our sins, and to gain all the indulgences we can. Most assuredly, those who pray regularly for the souls in purgatory will be less likely to go there themselves, or at least their time in purgatory will be shorter because of the way they live their lives.

34 What are Gregorian Masses for the faithful departed?

I have sometimes heard of people having "Gregorian Masses" offered for the soul of a deceased person. Could you please explain what this means and how a Gregorian Mass is different from any other Mass? Also, could these Masses be offered for living people?

The name "Gregorian Masses" comes from St Gregory the Great, who was Pope from 590 to 604 AD. Before becoming Pope, St Gregory had been a monk in a monastery which followed the rule of St Benedict. He tells in his fourth book of Dialogues of a monk in the monastery called Justus who, on becoming sick and approaching death, told his brother Copiosus where he had hidden three gold coins. When Gregory heard this, he was very grieved, especially since the rule of the monastery did not allow for the monks to have any property of their own.

Gregory then suggested to the prior that none of the monks should visit Justus in his sickness, so that he would be moved to repent of his sin. He also suggested that Justus' body not be buried with those of the other monks, but rather be put in some other place, along with the gold coins, as a lesson to the monks. When Justus was told why the others were not visiting him, he immediately sighed for his sin and expired.

A month later Gregory, moved by compassion, asked the prior to have 30 Masses said on consecutive days for the repose of Justus' soul. On the thirtieth day Copiosus had a vision in which his brother Justus told him that he was now in communion with God.

Copiosus went to the monastery to tell the monks what he had seen. Counting the days, the monks realised that the thirtieth Mass had been celebrated that very day. Copiosus was unaware that the Masses were being celebrated for his brother.

This is the origin of the "Gregorian Masses", which consist in 30 Masses being celebrated on consecutive days for the repose of the soul of a deceased person. The Masses themselves are no different from any other Mass and they need not use the liturgy of Masses for the faithful departed.

Naturally, one should not expect that just because the Masses are offered, the deceased person will necessarily be released from purgatory on the thirtieth day, if indeed he or she was there in the first place. It is up to almighty God, ever rich in mercy, to decide the length and intensity of punishment required for each soul before they are ready for heaven. At the same time, we can be sure that 30 Masses will be a big help in speeding souls on their way to eternal life. The problem these days is rather that people do not have enough Masses offered for their deceased relatives and friends, on the assumption that because they were good people they went straight to heaven.

Can Gregorian Masses, in the sense of 30 Masses on successive days, be offered for a living person? There is no reason why they cannot. The Mass can always be offered for the living or the dead.

35 How do our prayers help the souls in purgatory?

How do our prayers help the souls in purgatory? I always thought that the length of their stay in purgatory was dependent on the state of their soul when they died and that our prayers cannot shorten that time. Can you please enlighten me?

It is true, as you say, that the length of time a soul must spend in purgatory, or the extent of their punishment there, is determined by the state of their soul at the moment of death. As we have seen, the soul needs to purified of three things in order to be able to enter heaven: temporal punishment owing for sin, bad habits and attachments caused by sin, and any lack of sorrow for venial sins.

Since at their death each person has a different amount of temporal punishment owing for their sins, a different number of bad habits and attachments and a different degree of lack of sorrow for venial sins, it is only right that each soul will have a different amount of time, or degree of suffering, in purgatory. But we should never forget that God, in his infinite mercy, demands much less punishment than our sins deserve. If it were not for his mercy, we would never get out of purgatory!

Returning to your question, if each soul's degree of suffering is determined at the moment of their death, how can our prayers help them? Again, it is a matter of the mercy of God, expressed through the Communion of Saints. Just as God, in his power and mercy, answers our prayers for others here on earth by shortening their sufferings, curing their illnesses more quickly, healing broken relationships, etc., so he can answer our prayers for the souls in purgatory by shortening their sufferings.

Pope Benedict, in his encyclical *Spe Salvi*, explains it like this:

> If 'purgatory' is simply purification through fire in the encounter with the Lord, Judge and Saviour, how can a third person intervene, even if he or she is particularly close to the other? When we ask such a question, we should recall that no man is an island, entire of itself. Our lives are involved with one another; through innumerable interactions they are linked together. No one lives alone. No one sins alone. No one is saved alone… So my prayer for another is not something extraneous to that person, something external, not even after death. In the interconnectedness of Being, my gratitude to the other – my prayer for him – can play a small part in his purification (SS, 48).

Indeed, over the centuries there have been numerous accounts of souls in purgatory appearing to people on earth and asking for their prayers. Often the souls relate how the prayers of those on earth helped them and prepared them for heaven.

Recently a man told me that he had had a clear vision of three deceased persons whom he recognised, standing at his bedroom door and asking: "Why are you not praying for us?" If we too had such a vision, we would pray much more for the souls in purgatory. We do not need to wait for such a vision.

St Josemaría Escrivá (1902-1975) had an interesting way of explaining how our prayers help the souls in purgatory. Starting from the fact that many souls there have many people praying for them and others have none, he came up with an explanation whereby all souls would benefit equally. He described the souls in purgatory as if in a queue, with some closer to the gate of heaven and others farther back. When a prayer or other good work was offered for a particular soul, all would take a step closer to heaven, so that no one was left without help. We cannot be certain that this is the case, but at least it makes a lot of sense.

36 Can the souls in purgatory pray for us?

I have heard people say that we can ask the souls in purgatory to intercede before God for us. Is this true?

The answer to your question is a most emphatic yes – the souls in purgatory can pray for us. This is easy to understand, beginning from the fact that we can help each other on earth by our prayers for one another. Although there is only one mediator between God and man, Jesus Christ, (cf. *1 Tim* 2:5) Jesus shares his mediating role with others, including ourselves. When we pray for others, our prayers pass through the powerful mediation of Jesus, and through him they reach the Father. I suspect we have all seen our prayers for others answered in remarkable and unexpected ways at one time or another.

If we can help one another on earth and we can help the souls in purgatory, there is no reason why the souls in purgatory cannot intercede for us here on earth. After all, we are all united through the Communion of Saints and the souls in purgatory are closer to God than we are, given that they are being purified of their sins and their love for God is growing all the time. It seems only natural, for example, that a mother who has died will be praying from purgatory for the loved ones she left behind on earth. Without any special divine help she can pray for the general needs of her family and of other loved ones. And if there are special needs that she was unaware of while on earth, God can grant her knowledge of these needs, just as he grants the saints in heaven knowledge of the needs of certain people on earth.

Only in terms of this special knowledge granted by God can we explain how prayers through the intercession of deceased persons, including saints and blesseds, have so often been answered by the working of miracles. St Catherine of Bologna, who was very devoted to the souls in purgatory, was certain that her prayers to the holy souls were answered. She writes: "I received many and very great favours from the saints, but still greater favours from the holy souls."

While the Church has not pronounced on this question in a formal way, numerous theologians have used the reasons just given to argue that the souls in purgatory can pray for us. Among them are St Robert Bellarmine, Francisco Suarez and St Alphonsus Liguori. St Alphonsus writes: "So the souls in purgatory, being beloved by God and confirmed in grace, have absolutely no impediment to prevent them from praying for us. Still the Church does not invoke them or implore their intercession, because ordinarily they have no cognisance of our prayers. But we may piously believe that God makes our prayers known to them" (*Great Means of Salvation*, Ch. I, III, 2). St Alphonsus also mentions St Catherine of Bologna who, "whenever she desired any favour had recourse to the souls in purgatory and was immediately heard."

Thus, when someone close to us dies, it is quite appropriate to pray both *for* them and *to* them. Apart from the help the souls in purgatory give us by praying for us, our prayers for them always sanctify us by uniting us more with God and increasing our trust in him. In this sense, the souls in purgatory help us by moving us to pray for them.

37 Do souls in purgatory know we are praying for them?

I pray a lot for the souls in purgatory, but I have often wondered whether there is any evidence that the souls in purgatory know we are praying for them?

Gerard van den Aardweg, the Dutch psychologist I have quoted before, has an Epilogue in his book *Hungry Souls* which relates the repeated apparitions of a man to his daughter. It answers your question and many more.

The man died in 1870 and appeared numerous times to his daughter, Sister Mary Seraphine, a nun in Malines, Belgium. The account of the apparitions was first published in 1872, and then in 1895 it was included by J.A. Nageleisen in his book *Charity for the Suffering Souls: An Explanation of the Catholic Doctrine of Purgatory* (reprinted by TAN Books, Rockford 1982).

On 27 July 1870 Sr Mary received a letter from France informing her that her father had died on July 17. From that time on she often heard sounds of moaning like those of her father in his illness, and a voice crying out, "Dear daughter, have mercy on me, have mercy on me, have mercy on me!" On October 14, when she was about to fall asleep she saw her father standing near her bed, looking very sorrowful and enveloped in flames. She felt as if the flames were scorching her too. From then on she saw her father every evening, except for a few days at the end, until he finally went to heaven.

When she asked her father if he was relieved by the many Masses being offered for him he answered yes, but that he also wanted the Stations of the Cross. He explained that the rest of his children thought he was already in heaven and weren't praying for him. This is confirmed by a letter they wrote to their sister: "Father died like a saint, and is now in heaven." Only Sr Mary and an old servant named Joanna were praying for him. So the souls in purgatory clearly know who is praying for them – and who is not. And it is another case of someone who was known to be very holy but who still had to spend some time in purgatory.

Her father explained on one occasion that it was not necessary for the sisters to pray continually for him: "Every work, even the least, performed in the state of grace and offered to God, is meritorious and of atoning value, and serves to lessen our punishment." He went on: "Oh, if people would know what purgatory is! They would suffer everything in order to escape it and to release the poor souls confined in it."

He explained that at first he was going to have to spend many years in purgatory, but through the intercession of Our Lady, to whom he had great devotion, his time was reduced to a few months. Nonetheless, his suffering was so intense that he said in October, "If I shall have to remain in purgatory three months more it will seem an eternity." On October 30 he said: "Alas, the world does not believe that the fire of purgatory is similar to that of hell. If a person could but once visit purgatory, he would never more commit the least sin, so rigorously are the souls punished."

In answer to Sr Mary Seraphine's explicit questions as to whether the souls in purgatory know who prays for them and whether they are permitted to pray for the faithful on earth, he answered yes to both.

He explained that, having seen the infinite majesty of God, the sacred humanity of Christ and the Blessed Virgin Mary in his particular judgment, he felt a continuously increasing and ardent longing to see them again. He said that St Joseph, Our Lady and his guardian angel often visited purgatory to comfort him.

Finally, during Midnight Mass on Christmas Eve the man appeared to Sr Mary in great radiance and said: "My punishment is ended. I come to thank you and your community for all the prayers said for me. From now on I shall pray for you all."

Let us pray very much for all those who have died. In that way, not only do we help them but they can also pray for us. And we can be sure that if we go to purgatory ourselves, by the mercy of God there will be many people to pray for us.

Heaven

38 What is heaven like, and might it boring?

I was trying to explain the joy of heaven to my daughter recently and, among other comments, she said she would like to go to heaven but that it sounded boring. How can I answer her?

Let me first explain the Church's teaching on heaven and then I will answer the question of whether it might be boring. We can begin by looking at what Scripture has to say. St John writes that in heaven we shall see God as he is: "Beloved, we are God's children now; it does not yet appear what we shall be, but we know that when he appears we shall be like him, for we shall see him as he is" (*1 John* 3:2). St Paul is more graphic, saying that "now we see in a mirror dimly, but then face to face" (*1 Cor* 13:12). So heaven consists in being with God and seeing him "face to face".

Moreover, in heaven we will "see" not only God in the three divine Persons, but also the Blessed Virgin Mary, the angels and all the saints; that is, all the people who have finished their earthly journey and are now enjoying eternal life with God. When we say "see" we are referring to a vision that is not done with the eyes, since we will not have our body when we arrive in heaven. The spiritual soul will be able to "see" God and the other spiritual beings through a special help from God that St Thomas Aquinas and other theologians call the "light of glory" (cf. *STh* I, 12, 5). This light is a perfection of the intellect, as are the light of reason and the light of faith, so that the intellect can know God as he is in himself.

The Church's teaching on heaven is summarised in the *Catechism of the Catholic Church*: "This perfect life with the Most Holy Trinity – this communion of life and love with the Trinity, with the Virgin Mary, the angels and all the blessed – is called 'heaven'. Heaven is the ultimate end and fulfilment of the deepest human longings, the state of supreme, definitive happiness" (*CCC* 1024). Heaven is the fulfilment of our deepest longings. Man was made for love, for happiness, and he finds his complete fulfilment in the infinite love of God, who alone can satisfy this longing. This is what St Augustine had in mind when he wrote: "You have made us for yourself, and our heart is restless until it rests in you" (*Conf.* 1, 1, 1).

Our human experience bears this out. We search for happiness and, to a greater or lesser extent, we find it here on earth. But such happiness never satisfies us completely, nor is it lasting – it waxes and wanes over time. In heaven, on the contrary, our happiness will be complete and everlasting. In the words of the Catechism, it is "the state of supreme, definitive happiness".

The happiness of heaven is so great that it cannot be described in human terms. The Catechism teaches: "This mystery of blessed communion with God and all who are in Christ is beyond all understanding and description. Scripture speaks of it in images: life, light, peace, wedding feast, wine of the kingdom, the Father's house, the heavenly Jerusalem, paradise: 'no eye has seen, nor ear heard, nor the heart of man conceived, what God has prepared for those who love him'" (*1 Cor* 2:9; *CCC* 1027).

Given all of this, heaven cannot possibly be boring. It will be the maximum of happiness. Pope Benedict XVI writes that eternal life "would be like plunging into the ocean of infinite love, a moment in which time – the before and after – no longer exists. We can only attempt to grasp the idea that such a moment is life in the full sense, a plunging ever anew into the vastness of being, in which we are simply overwhelmed with joy" (Enc. *Spe Salvi*, 12).

As Pope Benedict points out, the eternity of heaven is not infinite extension of time, which might suggest that it is boring. In heaven there is no time as we know it on earth, no before and after. It is somehow timeless, supreme, definitive happiness. With that description, there is no way that it could be boring! And it is worthwhile sacrificing everything and struggling for holiness so that one day we will be there with God forever.

39 How do we know there is a heaven?

I have a friend who is very sceptical about life after death and would like some sort of proof that heaven is real. He says no one has ever been in heaven and come back to earth to tell us about it. What can I tell him?

When it comes to "proof" we have to be very careful. What we can give is strong arguments for the existence of life after death, but these may or may not convince another person. It is the same with the existence of God, where in one sense his existence is staring us in the face in his wonderful work of creation, but this may not convince a sceptic or an atheist. The most convincing "proof" for the existence of life after death is arriving there and seeing that it is a reality. But then it may be too late!

Coming back to your question, the following considerations may prove helpful. The first is that there *are* people who have been in heaven and have come back to earth to tell us about it. The most important is Jesus Christ himself who, as the Son of God, was in heaven from all eternity with the Father and the Holy Spirit and then came to earth as man. He spoke often of life after death, of judgment, heaven and hell. But why should a sceptic believe that Jesus is God who has come to earth? After all, he was the son of a carpenter from Nazareth and he died crucified in Jerusalem.

Well, we have multiple testimonies about Jesus in some very ancient writings, written only some twenty or thirty years after his death. They are, of course, the Gospels. They tell us that Jesus not only claimed to be God but showed that he was God by such remarkable feats as raising three people from the dead, curing a man born blind and prophesying his own death and resurrection, which came to pass.

St Paul too had a vision of heaven (cf. *2 Cor* 12:2-4) and came back to tell us about it. He found heaven indescribably beautiful and could only write: "What no eye has seen, nor ear heard, nor the heart of man conceived, what God has prepared for those who love him" (*1 Cor* 2:9).

If the sceptic wants more recent "proof" of heaven from someone who has been there, we can tell him about Our Lady, who was taken to heaven in the first century and has appeared on earth numerous times since then, bringing about miracles that admit of no human explanation. Consider, for example, the image she left at Guadalupe in Mexico in 1531 imprinted miraculously on a cactus fibre cloak, which has baffled scientists as to its origin and preservation, not to mention some of the details on it. Or Mary's apparitions in Fatima in 1917, where she told the three children several months beforehand that on October 13 she would work a great miracle. In fact on that day the miracle of the sun was seen by some 70,000 people. If there is no life after death or heaven, how is it that someone who died two thousand years ago can appear on earth and bring about such prodigious works?

One can also speak about the numerous miracles approved by the Church, which came about in answer to prayers to deceased people. Every beatification and canonisation requires two authenticated miracles and some of these are truly remarkable. If there is no life after death, how is it that prayers to a person who no longer exists can have any effect?

And then there are the numerous testimonies of people who have died, or almost died, and who have experienced the judgment and have seen heaven and hell. One of the most remarkable and well-known is that of Gloria Polo, a Colombian dentist who in May, 1995, was struck by lightning, suffered a cardiac arrest and was badly burned inside and out. She saw her lifeless body on a stretcher in the operating room. She had died in mortal sin and was taken by demons to hell to see what she deserved for her sins. Then she saw the terrible suffering of the souls in purgatory, the joy of souls in heaven, and finally her own judgment, in which she was condemned to hell. The sins that condemned her most included aiding and participating in abortion, receiving holy communion in a state of mortal sin, fortune-telling, and speaking evil of priests. She was given a second chance and came back to life on condition that she share her experience with others. She has done this all over the world and on the internet, writing her account in the book *Struck by Lightning: Death, Judgment and Conversion.*

Yes, there is life after death. There is a judgment, hell, purgatory and heaven and we should do everything possible to prepare ourselves for it. Now, before it is too late.

40 Where is heaven?

One question I have wondered about for a long time is "Where is heaven?" If there are bodies in heaven, as we know there are, at least in the case of Our Lord and Our Lady, then surely they must be somewhere in space, as we are. Is that the case?

The short answer to your question is no, that is not the case. Let's see if we can explain and understand this, as it is a bit tricky.

As you imply, if there are bodies anywhere in the universe, their position in space can be known and described with reference to all other bodies. They might be light-years away from each other, but we can define their position and know in which direction we must travel, and for how long, to get to them. This is the case for all material bodies. So, if in heaven bodies are like that, we should be able to know where they are in the universe and travel to them, perhaps in a spaceship. Then we could go to heaven while we were still alive. And everyone could go to heaven. Obviously, there is something wrong with this.

Part of the reason is that the bodies in heaven, including those of Jesus and Mary, are not material bodies. They were material when they were on earth, but now they are spiritual. We see this, for example, in the case of Jesus' body after the resurrection. While his risen body bore the wounds of the crucifixion and he could eat food, he could also suddenly appear and disappear, as he did with the disciples of Emmaus (cf. *Luke* 24:13-31), and he could pass through closed doors, as he did when he appeared to the apostles in the Upper Room in the evening on Easter Sunday (cf. *John* 20:19-20).

So too, Our Lady, in her numerous apparitions on earth throughout history, suddenly appears and then disappears. The people to whom she appears see her with their eyes, and she can speak their language, but if they approached her and tried to touch her, they would not feel a material body. Her body, like that of Christ, is spiritual, not material.

A good way to unravel this conundrum is to ask where God is. If heaven is the state in which we see God face to face, then heaven is where God is. But where is God? Again, when we ask that, we are inclined to think in terms of space as we know it on earth, the space where material bodies are, where the universe is. But God is not in that space. He is pure spirit, and he is in a different realm altogether, the spiritual realm. It transcends the physical universe.

The Catechism explains this difficulty in talking about any aspect of God, including where he is: "Since our knowledge of God is limited, our language about him is equally so. We can name God only by taking creatures as our starting point, and in accordance with our limited human ways of knowing and thinking" (*CCC* 40).

Since we creatures exist in time and space, we tend to think that God must be in time and space too. But he is not. He is not in time, where there is a before and after, but rather in eternity, where everything, the past, present and future, is present to him all at once.

Nor is God in space as we know it. God, being spiritual, is in another, spiritual, realm of existence. When we ask the question "Where is God?" in children's catechisms, we answer that "God is everywhere". But this "everywhere" does not mean everywhere in space as we know it. God's "space" is spiritual. Therefore, God cannot be located in terms of physical bodies in our own universe. This is a mystery, but it is something we must simply accept because it is a reality.

The Catechism puts it like this: "God transcends all creatures. We must therefore continually purify our language of everything in it that is limited, image-bound or imperfect, if we are not to confuse our image of God – the inexpressible, the incomprehensible, the invisible, the ungraspable – with our human representations" (*CCC* 42).

God is outside the space of material bodies, in a realm of his own. We say that God is everywhere, not in a spatial sense but in a spiritual sense. He is everywhere by his providence, guiding all beings to their end. He is everywhere by his knowledge, knowing everything and everyone, no matter where they are. He is present everywhere by his power, holding everything in being, having created everything out of nothing.

So God, and heaven, are in the spiritual realm, not in the physical realm of our universe. Since heaven is spiritual, we cannot go there by physical means. We can go to heaven only by spiritual means. That is, we must live a good life, be sorry for all our sins, make up for those sins either on earth or in purgatory, and then God will take us to be with him in heaven.

There we will experience the indescribable joy of being with the Blessed Trinity, Our Lady, the angels and all the saints, overwhelmed by God's love, with our desire for happiness completely satisfied. As the Catechism puts it, "Heaven is the ultimate end and fulfillment of the deepest human longings, the state of supreme, definitive happiness" (*CCC* 1024).

41 Is heaven only on earth?

I recently read an article which said that heaven, where souls go to enjoy God forever after their death and purification, will be only on earth when Christ comes again to inaugurate the new heaven and new earth. I thought we would go to heaven when we die. What are we to believe?

The Church's teaching on heaven is very clear. Yes, there will be a new heaven and a new earth when Christ comes again, and there will be a resurrection of the body on the last day, but all of this will not be on earth. It will be in heaven. Let me explain.

We find numerous statements on the question in the *Catechism of the Catholic Church*. For example, in the section on the resurrection of the body we read: "We firmly believe, and hence hope that, just as

Christ is truly risen from the dead and lives for ever, so after death the righteous will live for ever with the risen Christ and he will raise them up on the last day" (*CCC* 989). That is, immediately after their death the righteous will begin their life with the risen Christ in heaven, not on earth. And then on the last day Christ will raise up the body to be reunited with the soul.

Also, "In death, the separation of the soul from the body, the human body decays and the soul goes to meet God, while awaiting its reunion with the glorified body" (*CCC* 997). Two phases are indicated here. In the first phase, after death the soul goes to meet God in heaven while the body decays on earth. In the second phase the soul will be reunited with the glorified body at the end of time.

The Catechism goes on to quote the first Preface of Christian Death in the Roman Missal: "When the body of our earthly dwelling lies in death we gain an everlasting dwelling place in heaven" (*CCC* 1012). That is, immediately after death, while the body remains on earth, the soul already gains an everlasting dwelling place in heaven.

In the section on life everlasting, the Catechism quotes the prayer of Final Commendation in the funeral liturgy: "May you live in peace this day, may your home be with God in Zion, with Mary, the virgin Mother of God, with Joseph, and all the angels and saints…" (*CCC* 1020). Again, the prayer is that the soul will live in peace "this day" and that it will be at home in Zion, in heaven, with God, Our Lady, the angels and the saints.

Another clear statement in the Catechism comes under the heading of the Particular Judgment: "The New Testament … repeatedly affirms that each will be rewarded immediately after death in accordance with his works and faith" (*CCC* 1021). The soul will be rewarded immediately after death, not having to wait until the end of time. In this context we could also quote Our Lord's words from the cross to the good thief: "Truly I say to you, today you will be with me in Paradise" (*Luke* 23:43).

One of the clearest teachings on the question is also in the section on the Particular Judgment: "Each man receives his eternal retribution in his immortal soul at the very moment of his death, in a particular judgment that refers his life to Christ: either entrance into the blessedness of heaven – through a purification or immediately – or immediate and everlasting damnation" (*CCC* 1022). Again, eternal retribution comes at the very moment of death. As we know, entry into heaven can be immediate or preceded by purification in purgatory, and entry into hell is immediate.

As regards heaven itself, the Catechism describes it in terms of a spiritual state of union with God, not of a heaven on earth: "This perfect life with the Most Holy Trinity – this communion of life and love with the Trinity, with the Virgin Mary, the angels and all the blessed – is called "heaven." Heaven is the ultimate end and fulfilment of the deepest human longings, the state of supreme, definitive happiness" (*CCC* 1024).

So, we won't have to wait until the end of the world and the Second Coming of Christ, whenever that might be, to enjoy heaven. It comes immediately after death. And it is the spiritual state of heaven as we know it.

42 Can someone be certain of going to heaven?

I have a born-again Christian friend who says she is certain she is going to heaven simply because she "has been saved", having taken Jesus as her Lord and Saviour. I am not so certain of my own salvation. Should I be?

The short answer is that we can never be *absolutely certain* of our eternal salvation as long as we are on earth. Even though we are living well now, we may one day go off the track, as did the apostle Judas. We probably know people who were living exemplary lives at one stage but who later seemed to lose their way.

Nonetheless, many born-again Christians say they are certain of their eternal salvation. Some even say that if a Christian is not one hundred percent certain, they are not saved at all. Many follow the "once saved, always saved" creed, by which they mean that once they have been justified or saved by God, they always remain saved and are certain of going to heaven.

We admire their confidence, but we have to admit that it is not backed up by Scripture nor by the magisterium of the Church. And it flies in the face of common sense and the experience of our human frailty. For example, if anyone was "saved" it was St Paul, who was converted by Our Lord himself and was led to a radical change of his life and to numerous sacrifices and sufferings in spreading the Gospel. Yet not even St Paul was certain of his salvation. He writes to the Christians of Philippi, "Not that I have already obtained this [resurrection from the dead] or am already perfect; but I press on to make it my own, because Christ Jesus has made me his own. Brethren, I do not consider that I have made it my own; but one thing I do, forgetting what lies behind and straining forward to what lies ahead, I press on towards the goal for the prize of the upward call of God in Christ Jesus" (*Phil* 3:12-14).

Likewise, he writes to the Corinthians of the need to struggle in order to win the prize: "Every athlete exercises self-control in all things. They do it to receive a perishable wreath, but we an imperishable. Well, I do not run aimlessly, I do not box as one beating the air; but I pommel my body and subdue it, lest after preaching to others I myself should be disqualified" (*1 Cor* 9:25-27). If even the great Apostle of the Gentiles considers that he could still be disqualified, all the more should we.

Aware of his own frailty, St Paul warns the early Christians to be on guard: "Therefore, let any one who thinks that he stands take heed lest he fall" (*1 Cor* 10:12). Likewise, he cautions them not to take it for granted that they are saved, but rather "work out your own salvation with fear and trembling" (*Phil* 2:12).

Only at the end of his life, in his second imprisonment in Rome, is St Paul confident of his eternal salvation: "For I am already on the point of being sacrificed; the time of my departure has come. I have fought the good fight, I have finished the race, I have kept the faith. From now on there is laid up for me the crown of righteousness, which the Lord, the righteous judge, will award to me on that Day, and not only to me but also to all who have loved his appearing" (*2 Tim* 4:6-8).

In answer to the Protestant belief that a person can be certain of his eternal salvation, the Council of Trent teaches: "No one, moreover, so long as he lives this mortal life, ought in regard to the sacred mystery of divine predestination, so far presume as to state with absolute certainty that he is among the number of the predestined, as if it were true that the one justified either cannot sin any more, or, if he does sin, that he ought to promise himself an assured repentance. For except by special revelation, it cannot be known whom God has chosen to himself" (Sess. 6, Ch. 12).

It is for this reason that we are always advised to pray with hope and trust in God for the gift of final perseverance. The Council of Trent declared: "Similarly with regard to the gift of perseverance, of which it is written, 'He that shall persevere to the end, he shall be saved' (*Matt* 10:22), which cannot be obtained from anyone except from him who is able to make him stand who stands (*Rom* 14:4), that he may stand perseveringly, and to raise him who falls, let no one promise himself herein something as certain with an absolute certainty, though all ought to place and repose the firmest hope in God's help" (Sess. 6, Ch.13).

If we continue to struggle with humble trust in God, who gives everyone sufficient grace to be saved (cf. *2 Cor* 12:9), we can be confident, if not absolutely certain, of our salvation.

43 Is everyone equally happy in heaven?

I have always wondered whether the saints in heaven all experience the same degree of happiness, or whether some are more happy than others. Has the Church taught anything on this?

Your question is not just an idle query about an academic matter. The answer has a great bearing on how we live our lives here on earth. If everyone will receive the same reward in heaven some people will be tempted to ask: "Then what is the point of making an extra effort to do more, if we are not going to be rewarded for it? We may as well do the minimum and stay out of mortal sin so that at least we get to heaven, where we will receive the same reward as everyone else."

Has the Church said anything about this? It has. It has taught that each person will be rewarded differently in heaven, according to their works.

We can begin with Scripture, where we listen to Jesus himself. Speaking of the final Judgment, he says: "For the Son of man is to come with his angels in the glory of his Father, and then he will repay every man for what he has done" (*Matt* 16:27). And St Paul writes: "He who plants and he who waters are equal, and each shall receive his wages according to his labour" (*1 Cor* 3:8). Speaking of the glory of the resurrected body, he says: "There is one glory of the sun, and another glory of the moon, and another glory of the stars; for star differs from star in glory. So is it with the resurrection of the dead" (*2 Cor* 15:41-42).

Ludwig Ott, in his book *Fundamentals of Catholic Dogma*, lists as a dogma of faith the following proposition: "The degree of perfection of the beatific vision granted to the just is proportioned to each one's merits" (Tan, Rockford 1974, p. 479). The Council of Florence (1439), in the Decree *pro Graecis* declared that the souls of the perfectly just "clearly behold the Triune and One God as he is, but corresponding to the difference of their merits, the one more perfectly than the other" (*DS* 693).

In the sixteenth century, the Council of Trent taught that God will reward the good works of the justified person, always remembering that these good works are carried out through the grace and merits of Jesus Christ. The Council recalled the promise of Jesus: "And whoever gives to one of these little ones even a cup of cold water because he is a disciple, truly, I say to you, he shall not lose his reward" (*Matt* 10:42; Sess. 6, Ch. 16). The Council went on to define as a dogma of faith the following proposition: "If anyone says that ... the one justified by the good works that he performs by the grace of God and the merit of Jesus Christ, whose living member he is, does not truly merit an increase of grace, eternal life ... and also an increase of glory, let him be anathema" (Can. 32).

It is clear from this that there are different degrees of glory or perfection of the saints in heaven, depending on the merit of their good works on earth. This is only to be expected. God would be unjust if he did not reward some more than others, according to their works. We all expect that Our Lady, St Joseph, the Apostles, the martyrs and so many other "great saints" will be somehow "higher" in heaven than the rest of us. It would not be right if it were otherwise.

But does this mean that some will be happier in heaven than others? Not necessarily. In heaven all the saints are completely happy, overwhelmed by the love and glory of the Blessed Trinity, and in addition by the joy of being in the company of Our Lady, the angels, the other saints and their loved ones.

An analogy that is often given is vessels of different sizes, all full to the brim. By our good works we increase, as it were, the size of our vessel so that our capacity for love and happiness increases. In heaven, everyone's vessel will be completely full, so that all will be completely happy and no one will have a sense of lacking anything. And there will be no envy of others' happiness or glory since everyone will regard others' good as their own.

So there is every reason to make an effort to do all the good we can on earth, to store up as much treasure as we can in heaven (cf. *Matt* 5:19). Then, in addition to the reward we receive here on earth, we will also receive a greater reward in heaven. But it is important always to act for the highest motive: the love of God and our neighbour. The increase in happiness in heaven will follow as a consequence.

44 Where did the good people of the Old Testament go when they died?

> *I have always wondered where good people from the Old Testament like Abraham or Moses went after they died. It seems they could not go to heaven because Christ had not yet redeemed them from original sin, but they should not have gone to hell either.*

This is a frequently-asked question and the answer given by the medieval theologians is that the good people of the Old Testament went to what they called the "Limbo of the Fathers". The word "limbo" means a border and it is used here to refer to the border of heaven.

As you say in your question, as a consequence of the original sin of our first parents it was not possible for anyone to go to heaven until Christ came to redeem humankind. We see this in the fact that Adam and Eve were banished from the garden of Eden and angels were posted there so no one could enter (cf. *Gen* 3:22-24). This is a dogma of faith defined in two ecumenical councils, the Second Council of Lyons (1274) and the Council of Florence (1438). Those councils declared: "The souls of those who die in original sin as well as those who die in actual mortal sin go immediately into hell, but their punishment is very different" (*DS* 464, 693).

The word "hell", as used here, is a translation of the Latin word *infernum*, meaning the "lower region" or the "realm of the dead", not the hell of the damned. It means the state of deprivation of the Beatific Vision of heaven. That is why the councils say, "but their punishment is very different". The souls of the just who were in original sin suffered only the loss of the Beatific Vision and were very happy, while the souls of the damned suffered in addition the eternal pains of hell.

Among those in the "Limbo of the Fathers" would be the many figures of the Old Testament like the ones you mention, but also people from the time of Christ like the parents of Our Lady, Saints Joachim and Anne, St Joseph and St John the Baptist.

After Jesus died on the cross to redeem us from original sin, his soul went into the realm of the dead while his body remained in the tomb. It is of this that we speak when we say in the Creed that "he descended into hell" or "he descended to the dead". According to the Tradition, he went to the realm of the dead, or the "Limbo of the Fathers", to announce the good news of redemption to the souls detained there.

For example, St Ignatius of Antioch, who died in 107, writes to the Magnesians that Christ "awakened the prophets from the dead, who were his disciples in spirit, and who awaited him as their teacher on his arrival" (*Magn.* 9, 2). St Irenaeus, later in the second century, quotes an apocryphal passage from the prophecy of Jeremiah, in which he sees Christ's descent to the dead foretold: "The Lord, the Holy God of Israel, thought of his dead who slept in the earth of the grave, and he went down to them in order to announce to them the salvation" (*Adv. haer.* IV, 33, I, 12, and V, 31, I).

In the thirteenth century, St Thomas Aquinas wrote in the *Summa Theologiae*: "Consequently, when Christ descended into hell, by the power of his Passion he delivered the saints from the penalty whereby they were excluded from the life of glory, so as to be unable to see God in his essence, wherein man's beatitude lies, as stated in the I-II, 3, 8. But the holy Fathers were detained in hell for the reason that, owing to our first parent's sin, the approach to the life of glory was not opened. And so when Christ descended into hell he delivered the holy Fathers from there (*STh* III, 52, 5).

The *Catechism of the Catholic Church* sums up this teaching: "It is precisely these holy souls, who awaited their Saviour in Abraham's bosom, whom Christ the Lord delivered when he descended into hell" (*CCC* 633).

45 Can unbaptised infants go to heaven?

I have had two miscarriages and am wondering whether these babies might have gone to heaven. Does the Church have any official teaching on this?

You do well to ask whether the Church has an official teaching on the salvation of unborn babies since, strictly speaking, it does not. This is the question of what has traditionally been called Limbo, a state of natural happiness where infants would be very happy but they would not see God, as they would in heaven.

The idea of Limbo came from theologians, who started from Christ's words to Nicodemus: "Truly, truly, I say to you, unless one is born of water and the Spirit, he cannot enter the kingdom of God" (*John* 3:5). These words imply that some form of Baptism is necessary for salvation. In the case of adults, the Church has always taught that this can be Baptism of desire. This desire can be either explicit, as in the case of catechumens, that is those who have expressed a desire to be baptised, or implicit, in the case of those who are leading a good life and would choose baptism if they knew about it. Since infants cannot have this desire, the theologians concluded that if they are not baptised with water they cannot go to heaven. But neither are they deserving of hell. Therefore, they must be in a state of natural happiness, much greater than our happiness here on earth, but without the joy of seeing God face to face. This is what theologians called the "Limbo of children".

Over the centuries, different views have been expressed to explain possible ways by which unbaptised infants could still go to heaven. For example, St Thomas Cajetan OP (1469-1534) spoke of vicarious baptism of desire, where the infant would be saved through the desire by the parents or the Church of the child's Baptism. Heinrich Klee (1800-1840) spoke of infants being given the use of reason at the moment of death so that they could choose for themselves for or against God. And Herman Schell (1850-1906) suggested that the suffering and death of the infant was a sort of "quasi-sacrament", so that the infant would be saved by a "Baptism of suffering".

More recently, the then Cardinal Ratzinger, Prefect of the Congregation for the Doctrine of the Faith, said in *The Ratzinger Report*: "Limbo was never a defined truth of faith. Personally – and here I am speaking as a theologian and not as Prefect of the Congregation – I would abandon it since it was only a theological hypothesis. It formed part of a secondary thesis in support of a truth which is absolutely of first significance for faith, namely, the importance of Baptism. To put it in the words of Jesus to Nicodemus: 'Truly, truly, I say to you, unless one is born of water and the Spirit, he cannot enter the Kingdom of God' (*John* 3:5). One should not hesitate to give up the idea of 'Limbo' if need be (and it is worth noting that the very theologians who proposed 'Limbo' also said that parents could spare the child Limbo by desiring its Baptism and through prayer); but the concern behind it must not be surrendered. Baptism has never been a side issue for faith; it is not now, nor will it ever be" (p. 147).

The *Catechism of the Catholic Church* expresses the hope that unbaptised infants can be saved: "As regards *children who have died without Baptism*, the Church can only entrust them to the mercy of God, as she does in her funeral rites for them. Indeed, the great mercy of God who desires that all men should be saved, and Jesus' tenderness toward children which caused him to say: 'Let the children come to me, do not hinder them,' (*Mark* 10:14) allow us to hope that there is a way of salvation for children who have died without Baptism. All the more urgent is the Church's call not to prevent little children coming to Christ through the gift of holy Baptism" (*CCC* 1261).

In 2004, Pope St John Paul II entrusted the International Theological Commission with the task of studying the possibility of salvation of unbaptised infants. On 19 January 2007 their report was made public by Cardinal William Levada, President of the Commission, with the approval of Pope Benedict XVI. Their conclusion is very similar to that expressed in the Catechism:

> Our conclusion is that the many factors that we have considered above give serious theological and liturgical grounds for hope that unbaptised infants who die will be saved and enjoy the beatific vision. We emphasise that these are reasons for prayerful hope, rather than grounds for sure knowledge... What has been revealed to us is that the ordinary way of salvation is by the sacrament of Baptism. None of the above considerations should be taken as qualifying the necessity of Baptism or justifying delay in administering the sacrament. Rather, as we want to reaffirm in conclusion, they provide strong grounds for hope that God will save infants when we have not been able to do for them what we would have wished to do, namely, to baptise them into the faith and life of the Church (International Theological Commission, "The hope of salvation for infants who die without being baptised", 19 January 2007, 102-103).

In summary, we have great hope that unbaptised infants can be taken to heaven by God, but we cannot be sure of it. Therefore, parents should always have their babies baptised as soon as possible after birth, so that they have the certainty of their salvation.

46 Can non-Catholics go to heaven?

I have a knowledgeable friend who quotes Popes and saints to try to convince me that there are no Muslims, Jews or even Protestants in heaven, because the Church teaches that outside the Church there is no salvation. Is he right?

The statement that outside the Church there is no salvation goes back to the early Church and it has been taught and clarified down the ages. But it must be properly understood, lest it lead to the radical conclusion of your friend that there are only Catholics in heaven.

Among the early Fathers who taught that outside the Church there is no salvation, St Fulgentius of Ruspe, around the year 500, is one of the strongest: "Not only all pagans, but also all Jews and all heretics and schismatics, who finish their lives outside the Catholic Church, will go into eternal fire..." (*On Faith, to Peter* 38.81).

As for Popes, Pope Eugene IV in the Bull *Cantate Domino* (1441), using the same terms as St Fulgentius, taught in an infallible definition: "The Most Holy Roman Church firmly believes, professes and preaches that none of those existing outside the Catholic Church, not only pagans, but also Jews, heretics, and schismatics can ever be partakers of eternal life, but that they are to go into the eternal fire 'which was prepared for the devil and his angels' (*Matt* 25:41) unless before death they are joined with her."

Anyone reading these texts might well be inclined to believe that there are no Muslims, Jews or Protestants in heaven, only Catholics. But this would mean that the immense majority of mankind would go to hell. Did Jesus become man and die on the cross for only a few, or does he truly want all to be saved and to come to the knowledge of the truth? (cf. *1 Tim* 2:4) It is clearly the latter.

But then how are we to understand the teachings of the Church we have just cited? We must understand them in light of the tradition that one can belong to the Church not only through Baptism with water but also through Baptism of desire. This desire can be either explicit, in the case of catechumens who are preparing to enter the Church, or implicit, in the case of non-Catholics of good will who strive to lead a good life and who follow the will of God as they understand it.

Already in the second century St Justin spoke of the latter: "Those who acted in accordance with what is universally, naturally and eternally good were pleasing to God and will be saved by Christ ... just like the righteous who preceded them" (*Dialogue with Trypho*, 45).

This teaching was stated officially by the Holy See in answer to the errors of Fr Leonard Feeney, S.J., who had been professor of theology at Boston College and chaplain of the St Benedict Center at Harvard from 1945 on. Fr Feeney taught literally that outside the Catholic Church there is no salvation and only Catholics can go to heaven.

To clarify the Church's teaching, the Holy Office, with the approval of Pope Pius XII, sent a letter to the Archbishop of Boston, Cardinal Richard Cushing, on 8 August 1949. It stated, among other things, that in order for someone to be saved, "it is not always required that he be incorporated into the Church actually as a member, but it is necessary that at least he be united to her by desire and longing. However, this desire need not always be explicit, as it is in catechumens; but when a person is involved in invincible ignorance God accepts also an implicit desire, so called because it is included in that good disposition of soul whereby a person wishes his will to be conformed to the will of God."

This teaching was solemnly declared in the Second Vatican Council in the following terms: "Those who, through no fault of their own, do not know the Gospel of Christ or his Church, but who nevertheless seek God with a sincere heart, and, moved by grace, try in their actions to do his will as they know it through the dictates of their conscience – those too may achieve eternal salvation" (*LG* 16).

So when we get to heaven – and let us pray that we will – we will find there not only our fellow Catholics but also people of all beliefs who lived and died well, helped by grace and saved by Christ, who sought to fulfil the will of God as they knew it. Thank God for that.

47 Can someone who has left the Catholic Church go to heaven?

Many years ago my brother, who was brought up Catholic, albeit without much formation, married a Protestant and ever since he has worshipped in a Protestant Church, where he is very active and convinced of his new beliefs. Can he still be saved?

At the outset we should remember that salvation is always a matter between an individual soul and God. Whatever judgments we may make about a soul's state and worthiness for salvation as a result of their decisions here on earth, in the end it is God who judges that soul and we should not presume to play God.

The Church has something to say about the matter in the Second Vatican Council's Dogmatic Constitution on the Church *Lumen gentium*: "This holy Council first of all turns its attention to the Catholic faithful. Basing itself on scripture and tradition, it teaches that the Church, a pilgrim now on earth, is necessary for salvation: the one Christ is mediator and the way of salvation; he is present to us in his body which is the Church. He himself explicitly asserted the necessity of faith and baptism (cf. *Mark* 16:16; *John* 3:5), and thereby affirmed at the same time the necessity of the Church, which men enter through baptism as through a door. Hence they could not be saved who, knowing that the Catholic Church was founded as necessary by God through Christ, would refuse either to enter it, or to remain in it" (*LG* 14).

The final words can sound harsh. They seem to say that someone who knows that the Catholic Church was founded as necessary for salvation and does not enter it or leaves it voluntarily cannot be saved. Naturally these words do not apply to the many Catholics who no longer attend Mass, or who do so only irregularly, but still regard themselves as Catholics. They have remained in the Church and form part of the family of the Church. Naturally, in order to be saved they must repent of their serious sins and be reconciled with God before they die.

Someone, on the contrary, who leaves the Church in order to embrace some other faith, be it Christian or non-Christian, has in fact refused to remain in the Church, so it would seem that in principle they cannot be saved. Nonetheless, we would have to ask, and God would ask in the judgment, whether they really understood the importance of being Catholic, whether they knew that the Church was necessary for salvation. As you say in your question, your brother did not have solid formation in the Catholic faith, so he could very well be in ignorance on this matter. It is likely that most, or at least many, Catholics who leave the Church and embrace some other faith do not fully understand the importance of what it means to be Catholic.

When, like your brother, they embrace some other Christian faith, it is likely that they think it really doesn't matter to which denomination they belong, as long as it is Christian. Most Christians do believe that salvation comes only through Christ, so these people are convinced that they are on the way to heaven, having taken Jesus as their Lord and Saviour.

The Second Vatican Council goes on to explain how the Catholic Church is related to these other Christians: "The Church knows that she is joined in many ways to the baptised who are honoured by the name of Christian, but who do not however profess the Catholic faith in its entirety or have not preserved unity or communion under the successor of Peter. For there are many who hold sacred scripture in honour as a rule of faith and of life, who have a sincere religious zeal, who lovingly believe in God the Father Almighty and in Christ, the Son of God and the Saviour, who are sealed by baptism which unites them to Christ, and who indeed recognise and receive other sacraments in their own Churches or ecclesial communities...; these Christians are indeed in some real way joined to us in the Holy Spirit..." (*LG* 15).

So in summary, we cannot judge whether any individual Catholic who leaves the Church and enters some other faith is saved. It is up to God to do that. What we can do is pray very much for them that they may find the truth and live in accordance with it. We can also speak with them about their situation and give them good reading matter. And, of course, their salvation is certain if they return to the Catholic Church and persevere in the faith.

48 Can atheists go to heaven?

I recently heard someone say that atheists can go to heaven. This surprised me no end. Is it true?

In principle atheists can go to heaven, but there are a number of issues to consider. As the advertisement for a special offer often says, "Conditions apply."

The first issue is what we mean by atheist. The word atheist means simply one who does not believe in God and it distinguishes the person from a theist, who does believe in God. But within the broad category of atheist there are many different attitudes and backgrounds. It is impossible to lump them all together as if they were all one. It might even be safe to say that there are as many types of atheism as there are atheists. Each one is unique.

Over the years atheists have come to divide themselves into many different types: explicit and implicit, positive and negative, strong and weak, theoretical and practical, etc. The last distinction is perhaps one of the most helpful. In simple terms a theoretical atheist is one who has taken a positive stand against the existence of God – he or she denies that God exists – whereas the practical atheist does not believe in God but has not explicitly rejected such belief. He or she simply lives as if there were no God. Often this state of mind is found in people who have not been taught about God. They have simply not heard of him or they have ignored him. They are indifferent to the question of God.

Another factor which is very important is what the atheist believes deep down, as distinct from what they proclaim to others. I suspect there are many atheists who proudly and defiantly proclaim there is no God, but who secretly wonder about God and have a residual belief in a higher power "out there" to whom they would turn in a time of crisis. This is very relevant to their eternal salvation.

Then too the issue of time is important. The person who today proclaims herself or himself to be an ardent atheist may have a big conversion tomorrow. A notable recent example is Professor

Antony Flew, a British philosopher who, after 50 years of professed atheism, including writing books on the subject, came to believe in God through scientific discoveries. He relates his conversion in the book *There is a God,* published in 2007. With these considerations in mind, we return to your question, can atheists go to heaven?

We can begin with the practical atheists, especially those who simply do not know about God and who therefore live their lives without him. The Second Vatican Council, in the Dogmatic Constitution on the Church *Lumen gentium* spoke of them expressly: "Nor shall divine providence deny the assistance necessary for salvation to those who, without any fault of theirs, have not yet arrived at an explicit knowledge of God, and who, not without grace, strive to lead a good life. Whatever good or truth is found amongst them is considered by the Church to be a preparation for the Gospel and given by him who enlightens all men that they may at length have life" (*LG* 16). As the Council makes clear, these people must be in this position through no fault of their own and they must strive to lead a good life. This includes being sorry for their sins. If they fulfil these conditions, they can be saved.

As regards theoretical atheists who say they do not believe in God or that there is no God, their eternal salvation is more difficult. It is hard to see how they could spend eternity in a loving relationship with the God they have rejected during their life.

In the end, what is necessary for anyone to enter heaven, including a professed atheist, is for the person to repent of their sins and accept God's merciful love (cf. *CCC* 1033). An atheist, especially one with a faint belief that there might be a God, could still do this and be saved. We can hope and pray that even the most convinced atheists today may be able to repent and believe in God before they die. Since only God knows the state of their soul when they die, we should make no judgment about their eternal salvation. We should always pray for them.

49 Do Catholics have any advantage in going to heaven?

In view of the teaching that anyone, of any religion, can be saved, is there any advantage in being a Catholic? Wouldn't it be easier to be a Buddhist, a Hindu or a Protestant, since our faith makes more demands on us than do other religions?

It is not a matter of finding a religion that makes fewer demands on its members. Such religions abound. It is a matter of finding a religion that comes from God himself and that teaches with divine authority the way to heaven. There is one such religion and it is the one Jesus himself gave us: the Catholic Church.

And yes, the Church does make demands on us, but at the same time it gives us all the help we need to live up to those demands. We are expected to attend Mass on Sundays and Holy Days, to observe certain days and seasons of penance, to love our neighbour as ourselves, to respect the life of the unborn child by not having an abortion, to be faithful to our spouse until death, etc. Of course this makes life harder for us. But it is the way, the truth and the life that leads to happiness here and hereafter.

What is more, the Church's teachings on issues like abortion, euthanasia and the permanence of the marriage bond are not something dreamed up by medieval Popes or councils and then imposed on us forever after. They are teachings based on the natural law, on the very nature of the human person, and as such they are applicable to all, whether Catholic or not. Since they are so fundamental to human flourishing, they help us live as decent human beings who respect one another, and a society which lives them is all the better for it.

For this reason we are grateful to Jesus Christ for leaving us a Church which has the assistance of the Holy Spirit to teach us faithfully down the ages the way to happiness in this life and the next. It is true that other religions are not as clear and demanding in their teaching but this only makes it harder for their followers to live the kind of life that will lead to their true good.

What is more, the Church not only teaches us the way to

happiness, it gives us in the sacraments the fulness of the means we need to live up to that teaching. Baptism gives us a share in God's own life, with the indwelling of the Blessed Trinity in the soul and the sanctifying grace to make us holy and pleasing to God. Confirmation confirms the grace of Baptism and strengthens us to live up to our commitments as Christians. The Eucharist, which we can receive every day if we want, is the daily nourishment of our soul. It unites us fully to Christ and makes it easier to be Christlike in our behaviour. Penance forgives our sins and sends us on our way cleansed and strengthened to begin the spiritual struggle again. The Anointing of the Sick strengthens us when we are in danger of death and prepares us for the passage to eternal life with God. Matrimony gives us the grace to be faithful to our commitments in marriage, and Holy Orders gives us sacred ministers to administer the sacraments, to teach us the truths of our faith, and to accompany us along the way.

Where would we be without these helps? We should remember that all people in the world, whether Catholic or not, have to struggle to avoid sinning. No one is immune to temptation or sin. But how much easier it is to win out when we have the clear teachings of the Church about right and wrong and we have the sacraments to strengthen us and cleanse us when we have fallen. All will be judged on how they have lived the basic precepts of morality and it is so much easier when we have the helps the Church gives us.

What is more, attendance at Mass on Sundays is not a burden but a big help to live a good life. In Mass we are surrounded by our fellow Catholics, who pray with us and for us in our struggles. We hear the Word of God, which reminds us of the basic truths about God, life after death, and life here on earth. We have a homily, which suggests practical ways to put into practice what we have heard in the readings and helps us struggle for holiness. We pray together with the priest and the congregation, bringing us closer to God, whom we worship and thank for all his blessings. And above all we receive Holy Communion, which makes us one with Christ.

In short, there is every advantage in being Catholic. Not for nothing do hundreds of thousands of people enter the Church at the Easter Vigil each year, many of them coming from faiths that make far fewer demands on their members. Thank God for the Church.

50 Is there time in heaven?

One thing that has always intrigued me is whether there is time, in the sense of before and after, in the "eternal" life of heaven. Can you answer this?

First, we should ask what we mean by time. Time is associated with change and is measured in terms of change, so that wherever there is change of any sort there is time. The simplest example is an hour glass, where the sand falls through a narrow opening from the upper part to the lower part, always taking the same amount of time to do so. Similarly, we measure our days by the earth revolving around its own axis and our years by the earth revolving around the sun.

God, as we know, exists outside of time in eternity, where everything is present to him at once. The classic definition of eternity comes from the Roman senator and philosopher Boethius, (ca. 480–524 AD). Eternity, he says, is "the instantaneously whole and perfect possession of unending life" (*De consolatione*, v). That God is outside of time is a great mystery for us. We cannot fathom how the God who created the universe billions of years ago and now watches over it in its constant sea of change is himself unchanging, outside of time. In God the whole of history is present simultaneously. It is as if someone unrolled a film that recorded the whole of history and God saw it, from beginning to end, in one glance.

So if we and the universe are in time and God is in eternity, in which of these modes of existence are those in heaven, both angels and men? St Thomas Aquinas in his *Summa theologiae* speaks of a third mode called the aeon, also known as the aevum or aeveternity. An aeon, he says, is defined as "the measure of immaterial substances", so that it applies to angels in the first place but also to human souls in heaven. As he puts it, the aeon "lies somewhere between eternity and time" (*STh* I, q. 10, art. 5). Aeveternity is the unchangeable existence of immaterial substances which have a beginning but no end.

But in the case of angels and souls in heaven there is, surprisingly, both unchangeability and change. St Thomas says that angels "combine unchangeable existence with changeability of choice at the natural level, and with changeability of thoughts, affections and, in their own fashion, places." That is, while their very existence is unchangeable, their activity changes. Therefore, St Thomas says that "time has a before and after, the aeon has no before and after in itself but can be accompanied by it, whilst eternity neither possesses a before and after nor can co-exist with it" (*ibid.*).

As a result, angels and the souls in heaven share in some way in all three modes of existence. In the words of St Thomas, "Inasmuch as their thoughts and affections display successiveness, immaterial creatures are measured by time... But as regards their natural existence they are measured by the aeon; and inasmuch as they contemplate God's glory they share in eternity" (*ibid.*).

We can understand this. Traditionally the Church has taught that the essential happiness of heaven consists in the "communion of life and love with the Trinity" (*CCC* 1024), where the soul shares in God's eternity and there is no before and after. But there is also the accidental happiness of being in the company of Our Lady, the angels, the saints and all our loved ones. As new souls enter heaven, those already there rejoice, and this implies change and hence time. Likewise, God can allow the souls in heaven to be aware of what is happening with their loved ones on earth, and this too implies time.

Pope Benedict XVI writes of this eternal life in his encyclical *Spe salvi*:

> 'Eternal', in fact, suggests to us the idea of something interminable, and this frightens us; 'life' makes us think of the life that we know and love and do not want to lose, even though very often it brings more toil than satisfaction, so that while on the one hand we desire it, on the other hand we do not want it. To imagine ourselves outside the temporality that imprisons us and in some way to sense that eternity is

not an unending succession of days in the calendar, but something more like the supreme moment of satisfaction, in which totality embraces us and we embrace totality—this we can only attempt. It would be like plunging into the ocean of infinite love, a moment in which time—the before and after—no longer exists. We can only attempt to grasp the idea that such a moment is life in the full sense, a plunging ever anew into the vastness of being, in which we are simply overwhelmed with joy (n. 12).

51 Do pets go to heaven?

Recently our pet cat died and my daughter asked me whether it would go to heaven so that she can be reunited with it one day. I didn't know what to tell her.

This is indeed a frequently-asked question, especially by children. The answer can begin by distinguishing two phases of life after death: the phase between the arrival of the soul in heaven and the end of the world, and the phase of the "new heaven and new earth" at the end of the world.

In the first phase, in principle, there are no bodies or animals. Only a being with an immortal, spiritual soul can go to heaven. This includes both angels and human beings. In this phase, the body does not go to heaven along with the soul, but remains on earth. Of course, Our Lord and Our Lady are in heaven in both body and soul, along with perhaps a few others, possibly including the prophet Elijah and St Joseph, but they are there with a spiritual body, not a material one.

I say "in principle" because many people who have had near-death experiences in which their soul went to heaven, described seeing beautiful landscapes with rolling hills, plants, clouds, etc. Perhaps there is a place for animals there too, although everything there would be spiritual, not material, as they are on earth.

In view of this, it is clear that there are no material bodies in heaven, including those of animals. But, someone might ask, do animals not have an immortal soul too, so that at least their soul might be in heaven? No, they do not. They have a soul, a principle of life, along with all other living things, including plants. But that soul is not spiritual. It is simply what is called the "form" of the matter of the body, making the body function as a single living organism. When the animal, or the plant for that matter, dies, the soul ceases to exist. There is no longer any principle of life, any form, and the matter disintegrates.

In humans, on the other hand, the soul is spiritual and has existence in its own right. By our spiritual soul we are able to think, to reason, to know immaterial concepts such as goodness and truth, to plan for the future, etc., something even the highest animals cannot do. This spiritual soul, because it has no matter, is immortal or indestructible. When humans die, the soul lives on and goes either to purgatory, heaven or hell.

But will our happiness in heaven not be somewhat lessened if our pets are not there with us? Not at all. The very question reveals a lack of understanding of the overwhelming joy of seeing the Blessed Trinity, Our Lady and all the angels and saints. Pope Benedict describes heaven as "like plunging into the ocean of infinite love... in which we are simply overwhelmed with joy" (Enc. *Spe salvi*, n. 12). And the Catechism says that heaven is the "fulfillment of the deepest human longings, the state of supreme, definitive happiness" (*CCC* 1024).

In heaven we will be so caught up in the love of God that we will not miss anyone or anything. Even if a close relative like a son or daughter, a parent or a brother or sister of ours did not go to heaven, our happiness would not be lessened.

When we turn to the second phase of existence, that of the "new heaven and new earth" at the end of time, there might just be animals and plants there, including pets. If there is a new earth in some fashion, presumably there could be on it the things we see on earth now, although they would be in some way spiritual, not material.

Nonetheless, St Thomas Aquinas argues that there will be no animals and plants in the new earth because they were created for the benefit of man's bodily needs, and man will no longer have an earthly, material body (cf. *STh, Suppl.*, q. 91, art. 5). While St Thomas is always to be taken seriously, this statement is not equivalent to a dogma of faith or an official teaching of the Church.

In all this it is important to help our children – and ourselves! – not to be "pet-centred", but rather God-centred: to love our pets, yes, but to love God much more. After all, the new earth will still be in heaven, where all is centred on God and his love.

52 Is it easy to go straight to heaven?

I have always thought that it is not easy to go straight to heaven when we die, but recently a friend argued, based on the Summa Theologiae *of St Thomas Aquinas, that the Anointing of the Sick removes all our temporal punishment and, in any case, there is a plenary indulgence at the moment of death for those who prayed habitually, so they would go straight to heaven. Is this true?*

We recall that in order to enter heaven the soul must be perfectly purified. The Letter to the Hebrews speaks of "that holiness without which no one will see the Lord" (*Heb* 12:14). And Our Lord uses the parable of the wedding garment, without which no one will be allowed into the wedding banquet of heaven (cf. *Matt* 22:1-14). In view of this, the *Catechism of the Catholic Church* teaches: "All who die in God's grace and friendship, but still imperfectly purified, are indeed assured of their eternal salvation; but after death they undergo purification, so as to achieve the holiness necessary to enter the joy of heaven" (*CCC* 1030).

For this reason the Church has, from the beginning, prayed and offered Masses for the faithful departed, no matter how holy they were. The prayers of the funeral Mass always ask God to have mercy on the person's soul and to take them to heaven. They do not assume that the person is already in heaven. And the Church dedicates the month of November to praying especially for the souls in purgatory, following the commemoration of All Souls on November 2. So it is clear that the Church herself does not assume that practically everyone goes straight to heaven.

What does St Thomas say about the effects of the Anointing of the Sick? He deals with the question in the Supplement to his *Summa Theologiae*, where he speaks of three consequences of sin which are healed in some way by the sacrament. The first is the guilt, or stain, of sin and this is taken away by the sacrament, at least as regards venial sins. Mortal sins must first be repented of and confessed before receiving the sacrament.

The second consequence is temporal punishment. As we have seen, every sin we commit, whether venial or mortal, requires that we do something to make up for it. We do this by all our good deeds, our prayers and sacrifices, and indulgences. This punishment is called temporal, from the Latin word for time, because it must be made up in time, either here on earth or in purgatory. St Thomas says that the Anointing "diminishes the debt of temporal punishment". It diminishes the debt, but it does not necessarily take it away completely.

The third consequence is what St Thomas calls the "remnants of sin" and these too are diminished. By remnants he means "a certain spiritual debility in the mind" such that when it is removed "the mind is not so easily prone to sin" (cf. *STh*, Suppl., q. 30, art 1).

As is clear, St Thomas in no way suggests that all the effects of sin, especially temporal punishment, are removed so that the soul would be able to go immediately to heaven after receiving the Anointing of the Sick. Baptism does remove all the temporal punishment but the Anointing of the Sick does not.

As regards the plenary indulgence granted by the Church at the moment of death, this too must be understood properly. As we know, a plenary indulgence removes all the temporal punishment owing for our sins, and the Church, as you say, grants a plenary indulgence at the moment of death to all those who "are properly disposed and have been in the habit of reciting some prayers during their lifetime" (Pope Paul VI, Apost. Const. *Indulgentiarum doctrina*, n. 18). Does this mean that since most Catholics have been in the habit of praying during their life, they will receive the plenary indulgence and go straight to heaven?

Not necessarily. First, they must be "properly disposed", meaning they must be in the state of grace and they must reject all attachment to sin, even venial sin. This rejection of attachment to sin may be difficult to do, since it requires a great love for God and with it an abhorrence of sin, even the slightest sins. But even if the plenary indulgence does take away all the temporal punishment owing for their sins, the person may still not be sorry for all their venial sins or they may still have bad habits and attachments caused by sin. Any of these would prevent their immediate entry into heaven.

So, while we can hope that many people do go straight to heaven, we should take nothing for granted and we should always pray and have Masses said for those who have died, no matter how good they were. It is better to offer prayers and Masses for someone who does not need them than to leave the person in purgatory without anyone to pray for them.

53 Can we ask Our Lady and the saints in heaven to pray for us?

My Protestant friends tell me we should not pray to Mary or the saints but only to Jesus, because he is the only mediator between God and man. What should I believe about this?

To justify their contention that we should not pray to the saints but only to Our Lord, our Protestant friends like to quote a passage from St Paul which says: "For there is only one God, and there is one mediator between God and men, the man Christ Jesus" (*1 Tim* 2:5). What are we to make of this?

Naturally, we accept Paul's words that there is only one mediator between man and God: Jesus Christ. As Jesus himself said: "No one comes to the Father but by me" (*John* 14:6). That is, we have access to the Father only through Jesus, the one mediator. All other mediators, including Mary and the saints, thus go to the Father through him.

But there is nothing to prevent Jesus from sharing his mediating role with others. The Second Vatican Council in the Dogmatic Constitution on the Church, *Lumen gentium*, with particular reference to Mary's mediating role, explains it like this:

> Therefore the Blessed Virgin is invoked in the Church under the titles of Advocate, Helper, Benefactress, and Mediatrix. This, however, is so understood that it neither takes away anything from, nor adds anything to, the dignity and efficacy of Christ the one Mediator. No creature could ever be counted along with the Incarnate Word and Redeemer; but just as the priesthood of Christ is shared in various ways both by his ministers and the faithful, and as the one goodness of God is radiated in different ways among his creatures, so also the unique mediation of the Redeemer does not exclude but rather gives rise to a manifold cooperation which is but a sharing in this one source. The Church does not hesitate to profess this subordinate role of Mary, which it constantly experiences and recommends to the heartfelt attention of the faithful, so that encouraged by this maternal help they may the more closely adhere to the Mediator and Redeemer" (*LG* 62).

Thus, when we pray to Mary or any of the saints, they can present our petitions to the Father through the mediation of Jesus. Even more, as the Council says, when we go to Mary's maternal help, we are actually drawn closer to Jesus, the Mediator and Redeemer. Mary's role, as the Council says, is subordinate to that of Jesus. In an earlier paragraph the Council had said: "[Mary's salutary influence on men] flows forth from the superabundance of the merits of Christ, rests on his mediation, depends entirely on it and draws all its power from it" (*LG* 60).

It is easy to understand how others can share in Jesus' unique mediating role. For example, whenever we pray for others we are acting as mediators between them and the Father. Even if we do not expressly ask Jesus to intercede, but rather pray directly to the Father, our prayers still reach the Father only through Jesus. Anyone who quotes Scripture to say that we do not need Mary, since Jesus is the only mediator, should be reminded that those same Scriptures tell us that Mary interceded before Jesus for a married couple at Cana when the wine had run out, and that Jesus did his first miracle as a result of her intercession (cf. *John* 2:1-11).

In short, yes, there is only one mediator, Jesus Christ, but others can share in his mediating role, including ourselves. If we can share in it, all the more can the saints in heaven, who are closer to God than we are.

To be sure, there is a very widespread and ancient custom of praying to Mary and the saints for our needs, and the Church encourages it. The Vatican's 2001 *Directory on Popular Piety and the Liturgy* says: "The doctrine of the Church and her Liturgy propose the Saints and Beati who already contemplate God in the 'clarity of his unity and trinity' to the faithful because they are ... intercessors and friends of the faithful who are still on their earthly pilgrimage, because the Saints, already enraptured by the happiness of God, know the needs of their brothers and sisters and accompany them on their pilgrim journey with their prayers and protection" (n. 211).

The saints are aware of our needs if God reveals our needs to them, and he can do this. St Thomas Aquinas, in the Supplement to his *Summa Theologiae* says that this is the case. Speaking of the saints in heaven, he says: "Now it pertains to their glory that they assist the needy for their salvation: for thus they become God's cooperators, *than which nothing is more Godlike*, as Dionysius declares (*Cael. Hier.* iii). Wherefore it is evident that the saints are cognizant of such things as are required for this purpose; and so it is manifest that they know in the Word the vows, devotions, and prayers of those who have recourse to their assistance" (*Suppl.* q. 72, art. 1). As St Thomas says, the saints in heaven know what is necessary in order to intercede for the needy on earth. And they know this "in the Word", in the Son of God, not directly by themselves.

We see the ancient custom of praying to the saints in the Church's numerous litanies which go through a long list of saints, asking each one in turn to "Pray for us". We are encouraged to pray to the saints too by the words of St Thérèse of Lisieux quoted in the Catechism: "I want to spend my heaven in doing good on earth" (*CCC* 956).

We can pray too to our recently deceased relatives and friends, who know our needs and can intercede for us, if God reveals these needs to them.

Perhaps the custom of praying to Our Lady and the saints follows an unexpressed, but implicit, thought that God is more likely to hear our petitions if they are presented to him by someone closer to him and more worthy than we are. We do this in our earthly affairs when we seek the help of intermediaries to ask an important person to help us, on the understanding that the intermediary is more likely to receive a favourable response than we are. The saints in heaven and even the souls in purgatory are much closer to God than we are, and so are powerful intermediaries.

As regards prayer specifically to Mary, various writers have expressed the thought that Jesus never said no to his mother while he was on earth and he won't say no to her in heaven. The miracle at Cana bears this out (cf. *John* 2:1-12).

What is more, the efficacy of prayer to the saints is seen in the long list of miracles attributed to their intercession for their causes of beatification and canonisation. So let us keep up our prayer to Mary and the saints. It is very powerful.

54 Do the saints in heaven feel sad for those in hell?

If a mother in heaven knows that her son did not go to heaven but went to hell, won't she somehow feel sad?

That is a frequently-asked question and it is not difficult to answer. We can start from Scripture, where the book of Revelation describes life in the New Jerusalem, or heaven, like this: "Behold, the dwelling of God is with men. He will dwell with them, and they shall be his people, and God himself will be with them; he will wipe away every tear from their eyes, and death shall be no more, neither shall there be mourning nor crying nor pain any more, for the former things have passed away" (*Rev* 21:3-4).

In heaven with God, all is joy, indescribable joy on seeing God face to face and being in the added company of Our Lady, the angels and all the saints. The Catechism says of heaven: "Heaven is the ultimate end and fulfillment of the deepest human longings, the state of supreme, definitive happiness" (*CCC* 1024).

Supreme happiness is incompatible with any sadness whatsoever, including the knowledge that a loved one is suffering in hell. To be in the presence of the Blessed Trinity and to experience the infinite love of God is to be overwhelmed with joy. There can be no sadness in heaven.

But then how can a soul in heaven be so happy if it knows that a loved one is in hell? The question presumes that the soul in heaven does know that a loved one is in hell. That is not certain. In principle, apart from the knowledge it has of everything around it in heaven, it can know only what God allows it to know. So do the saints in heaven know whether someone, including a loved one, is in hell? It may very well be that they do not. St Thomas Aquinas says: "Although it does not follow that those who see the Word see all things in the Word, they see those things that pertain to the perfection of their happiness, as stated above" (*Suppl.* q. 72, art. 1, Reply Obj. 4). Since the knowledge that someone they knew was in hell would not contribute to the perfection of their happiness in heaven, it is likely that they are unaware of this fact. After all, they are so caught up in the glory and love of God that they are unaware of anything outside of heaven that would detract from their supreme happiness.

What is more, since their happiness comes wholly from their relationship with God, it does not depend any longer on their relationship with persons on earth. If it did, their happiness would be lessened every time a loved one on earth was sick, or depressed, or anxious. Clearly this cannot be, and therefore even the fact that someone was suffering in hell would not detract from their happiness, if indeed they were aware of this fact.

In summary, in heaven there is only supreme happiness, never sadness.

55 Will we be reunited with family members in heaven?

My husband died this year, and I'm having a hard time adjusting to life without him. A friend said that I can expect to be reunited with him in heaven. Is this true?

I think we all have a deep desire to be reunited with our loved ones in heaven. And this desire will be satisfied, provided of course that both we and our loved ones go to heaven. The Catechism refers to this communion with all the blessed in heaven: "This perfect life with the Most Holy Trinity – this communion of life and love with the Trinity, with the Virgin Mary, the angels and all the blessed – is called 'heaven'" (*CCC* 1024). The word "communion" means just that. We will be in communion, in union, with all those in heaven. And it will be a communion "of love". We will love God and everyone else in heaven.

It is the traditional teaching of the Church that happiness in heaven is twofold: essential and accidental. The essential happiness is union with God in the Blessed Trinity, and the accidental happiness is union with all the others in heaven. These include Our Lady, St Joseph, the angels and all the other souls there. In heaven we will be intimately united with everyone else. It will be a great reunion of the family of the Church and of all mankind.

Our Lord alludes to it: "I tell you, many will come from east and west and sit at table with Abraham, Isaac, and Jacob in the kingdom of heaven…" (*Matt* 8:11). Christ often likened the kingdom of heaven to a wedding banquet, where people of all backgrounds will be united in love for the bridegroom and bride, and for one another.

Another expression of the union of all in heaven with God and with each other is the communion of saints. That communion includes all the blessed in heaven, the souls in purgatory and the baptised on earth. They are all united in one great communion, and they can all pray for one another. The saints in heaven and the souls in purgatory pray especially for those on earth to reach the goal of heaven.

But what happens if someone's first spouse died and they married someone else? Will they have two spouses in heaven? That is the question the Sadducees, who don't believe in the resurrection, asked Our Lord, to try to trap him and show him there can't be life after death. We remember his answer: "For in the resurrection they neither marry nor are given in marriage, but are like angels in heaven" (*Matt 22:30*). This can be understood in the sense that one's marriage, or marriages, on earth will not matter, as the focus of all in heaven will be on God. A person with several spouses will be united with all of them in the love of God. It is a wonderful reality.

In heaven, all is love, complete love. So any lack of love, any criticism or spite people may have had for one another on earth will be swallowed up in total love in heaven. Similarly, if someone finds himself in heaven with someone he positively despised on earth, that will not be a problem either. He will have been sorry for this lack of charity and will have purged the effects of that sin, so he will now love everyone intensely. There is no hatred or dislike in heaven. All is love, all is union.

A related question is how we will even recognise our loved ones in heaven, when neither they nor we will have a body, only a soul, until the resurrection of the body on the last day. How this will be we cannot know, but there are numerous accounts of people with near-death experiences whose soul went to heaven, where they recognised loved ones. There are also accounts of people on earth seeing with their eyes a deceased loved one. Often what they saw they described as a spiritual, heavenly face. In any case, we will find out about this reality when we go to heaven.

What is certain, though, is that we will be reunited with our loved ones in heaven. The final commendation of the funeral Mass confirms this truth: "There is sadness in parting, but we take comfort in the hope that one day we shall see N. again and enjoy his/her friendship."

56 How old will we be in heaven?

When we get to heaven, will we be of the same age as when we died or some other age?

St Thomas Aquinas answers that question in his *Summa Theologiae*. Naturally, he could only speculate about the answer, based on reason and Scripture, but what he says is plausible.

He first quotes St Paul's letter to the Ephesians: "Until we all meet ... unto a perfect man, unto the measure of the age of the fulness of Christ" (*Eph* 4:13). From this he concludes: "Now Christ rose again of youthful age, which begins about the age of thirty years, as Augustine says (*The City of God*, 22). Therefore, others also will rise again of a youthful age" (*STh*, Suppl. q. 81, art. 1).

St Thomas goes on to justify his conclusion: "Man will rise again without any defect of human nature, because as God founded human nature without a defect, even so will he restore it without defect. Now human nature has a twofold defect. First, because it has not yet attained to its ultimate perfection. Secondly, because it has already gone back from its ultimate perfection. The first defect is found in children, the second in the aged: and consequently in each of these, human nature will be brought by the resurrection to the state of its ultimate perfection, which is in the youthful age, at which the movement of growth terminates, and from which the movement of decrease begins" (*ibid*).

In fact, there is some anecdotal evidence for what St Thomas is saying. Consider, for example, the case of three-year-old American boy, Colton Burpo, who had a near-death experience of heaven, which I related in my book *Dying to Live – Reflections on Life After Death* (Connor Court 2022, p. 64). His story was popularised in the book and later the film *Heaven is for Real*. While undergoing surgery for a burst appendix in 2003, Colton's soul left his body and went to heaven, where he says he met his great-grandfather, who had died thirty years before Colton was born. His parents were naturally sceptical about how he could have known someone he had never met, so they showed him a photograph of his great-grandfather taken late in life. Colton said no, that was not the person he saw. Only when they showed him a photo of him as a young man did he recognise him.

Another case concerns Gabrielle, the wife of a friend of mine, who died of a heart attack in January 2014 at the age of 64. Some three years later, in December 2016, Michael, a well-known television journalist friend of her family, was in Mass in Sydney's St Mary's

Cathedral when he suddenly saw Gabrielle. As an investigative journalist, Michael was always sceptical about the truth of anything or anyone he was investigating. He describes what he saw in his book *A Sceptic's Search for Meaning*:

> "I have now had the most indescribable experience of seeing someone in heaven. I know that is a big statement and one which will be questioned by many. But my belief in the authenticity of this experience is unshakeable... It is an innocuous image of her that I see but, oh, so powerful: her full face, her hair and a hint of the top of her shoulders... I am stunned by how beautiful she is. She was a beautiful young woman when I first met her, but she was in her sixties when she died and her looks, as you'd expect, had changed. But there is not the slightest doubt in my mind that this is my friend, Gabrielle. She appears as if she is in her late twenties and her beauty is beyond what I had encountered in life: smiling quietly with a look of contentment and relaxation... I have trouble finding the words because the ones that come to mind, like 'beautiful', 'relaxed', and 'serene', don't seem sufficient. They are too common and overused. Then the right word comes to me in a jolt: 'heavenly'."

Six weeks after Gabrielle appeared to Michael, she appeared to a lawyer from Melbourne who was also a family friend. He said he was lying in bed when "a young and very beautiful woman appeared to me. I thought she was aged in her twenties. I could only see her from the shoulders upwards. Her face was beautiful. She was happy, peaceful and heavenly... I only knew Gabrielle when she was about 60 years of age. I did not know what she looked like in her twenties, but somehow, I knew it was definitely Gabrielle."

Admittedly, these are only anecdotes, but they do point to the possibility that we will all be young in heaven. We'll find out when we get there.

57 Will there be disabilities in heaven?

My little sister is blind and I am wondering if somehow she will be able to see God in heaven. Do we know anything about this? And how about other disabilities?

Before I venture to answer the question, it is important to recall the fundamental teaching about heaven, which applies to all the souls there, no matter what disabilities they may have had on earth. Heaven is "perfect life with the Most Holy Trinity – this communion of life and love with the Trinity, ... the ultimate end and fulfilment of the deepest human longings, the state of supreme, definitive happiness" (*CCC* 1024). The most important aspect of heaven is that everyone there will be supremely happy. Who wouldn't be happy, in the presence of God, Our Lady, the angels and all the saints?

At the same time, we should remember that when we arrive in heaven we will be there in our soul, not our body. Only with the resurrection of the body on the Last Day will we be "whole" again, body and soul. Nonetheless, many of the people who saw heaven during near-death experiences said they saw loved ones there, whom they recognised by their faces. That suggests that we may have some sort of "spiritualised" body in heaven.

The Catechism sheds further light on the question: "To live in heaven is 'to be with Christ.' The elect live 'in Christ', but they retain, or rather find, their true identity, their own name" (*CCC* 1025). So everyone will retain their own identity in heaven. We will be the same person there that we are here. On earth we identify ourselves by our personality, our memories, our body, our talents, our abilities and disabilities. People with disabilities do too.

It is important here to clarify what we mean by "disabilities". When we think of the word, we generally mean a lack of ability in some bodily or mental function. In that sense, we all have disabilities. We cannot all run as fast as an Olympian, or sing as well as an opera singer, or think as well as a university professor. We all have many lacks of ability. People with "disabilities" in the usual sense of the word, simply have more serious lacks of ability. They may not be able to walk without a limp or a mechanical aid, they may not be able to see or hear well, etc. But these are not moral defects. They are simply variations in the way God made us humans. Disabilities do not make a person less perfect, less pleasing to God.

At the same time, people with disabilities have many abilities, sometimes acquired with great effort. We admire them for their prowess in sport, so evident in the Paralympics, in their many talents, their success in various fields of work, in the arts, music, etc. Many have made great contributions to society. If asked whether they would like to be free of their "disability" in heaven, many would answer flatly no. Their disability is part of who they are. It is their identity. They just want to be themselves.

We all do. We will be in heaven the same person we are on earth, with all the variations of talents and abilities we have here. We will not all be clones of some "perfect human", whatever that might be. Even Christ appeared in his risen body with the wounds in his hands, feet and side that he suffered on earth (cf. *John* 20:24-29).

What we will not have, of course, is moral defects: sin and its consequences. Nor will there be pain or suffering, since God "will wipe away every tear from their eyes, and death will be no more, neither shall there be mourning nor crying nor pain any more, for the former things have passed away" (*Rev* 21:4). And all, even the blind, will see God "face to face" (*1 Cor* 13:12).

In short, in heaven we will be the same person we are now, enjoying "supreme, definitive happiness" (*CCC* 1024). And whatever disabilities we may have had on earth will be of no effect in heaven.

58 When did those who died before Christ go to heaven?

I remember a priest saying that the souls of the good people who died before Christ, like St John the Baptist and St Joseph, only went to heaven when Christ ascended there. Is this true?

While not a dogma of faith, the proposition you mention is a common teaching of the Church, a teaching which the Church has taught and believed for many centuries.

As background, we should remember that when Adam and Eve committed the original sin of disobedience to God's command not to eat of the fruit of a certain tree, heaven was closed and no one was able to go there. As we have seen, it is a common teaching of the Church that the good people who died before Christ, like the ones you mention, were in a state of natural happiness called the "Limbo of the Fathers" awaiting their Redemption, which took place when Christ died on the Cross and rose from the dead. When we say that Christ "descended into hell", or "he descended to the dead", we are referring to that state or place, where he went to announce the good news of Redemption.

The reason why we say that those souls only went to heaven when Christ himself did, is that he is the head of the Mystical Body and it is only right that the head should precede the body in entering heaven. In this regard the *Catechism of the Catholic Church* teaches: "Left to its own natural powers humanity does not have access to the 'Father's house,' to God's life and happiness. Only Christ can open to man such access that we, his members, might have confidence that we too shall go where he, our Head and our Source, has preceded us" (*CCC* 661).

Ludwig Ott, in his *Fundamentals of Catholic Dogma* writes: "From the soteriological angle it [the Ascension] is the crowning conclusion of the work of the Redemption. According to the general teaching of the Church, the souls of the just of the pre-Christian era also moved with the Saviour into the glory of Heaven." Ott cites as a reference St Paul's letter to the Ephesians, which in turn quotes Psalm 68: "When he ascended on high he led a host of captives, and he gave gifts to men" (*Eph* 4:8; cf. *Ps* 68:18; Ott, p. 194).

St Thomas Aquinas, in answer to the question, writes in the same vein:

> In regard to those things which, in ascending, he did for our salvation. First, he prepared the way for our ascent into heaven, according to his own saying (*John* 14:2): 'I go to prepare a place for you' and the words of Micah (2:13), 'He shall go up

that shall open the way before them.' For since he is our head, the members must follow where the head has gone; hence he said (*John* 14:3): 'That where I am, you also may be'. In the saints delivered from hell, according to *Ps* 68:18 (cf. *Eph* 4:8): 'Ascending on high he led captivity captive', because he took with him to heaven those who had been held captives by the devil, to heaven, as to a place strange to human nature; captives indeed of a happy taking, since they were acquired by his victory" (*STh* III, q. 57, art. 6).

Catholic doctrine on this subject was stated authoritatively by Pope Benedict XII in his Apostolic Constitution *Benedictus Deus* (1336):

> By this Constitution, which is to remain in force for ever, we, with apostolic authority, define the following: According to the general disposition of God, the souls of all the saints who departed from this world before the passion of our Lord Jesus Christ [...] since the ascension of our Lord and Saviour Jesus Christ into heaven, already before they take up their bodies again and before the general judgment, have been, are and will be with Christ in heaven, in the heavenly kingdom and paradise, joined to the company of the holy angels.

How then can we explain Our Lord's words from the Cross to the good thief: "Today you will be with me in paradise" (*Luke* 23:43)? Since "with the Lord one day is as a thousand years" (*2 Pet* 3:8), Christ was not referring to that particular day, Good Friday, but rather to the "today" of God's time. The good thief no doubt went to heaven, along with all the other good people of the Old Testament, on the day of Christ's Ascension.

The Last Day

59 What do we mean when we speak about the Last Day?

I hear people these days speaking of preparing for the "end times", as if the end of the world is coming soon. They disturb me. What does the Bible say about the Last Day?

According to the Church's tradition, on the Last Day a number of events will take place. The world will come to an end, Christ will come again in glory, in his Second Coming, sometimes called the Parousia, to judge the world in the Last Judgment, the bodies of the dead will be resurrected and reunited with their souls, and the new heavens and new earth will begin.

As regards the end of the world, St Peter writes: "But the day of the Lord will come like a thief, and then the heavens will pass away with a loud noise, and the elements will be dissolved with fire, and the earth and the works that are upon it will be burned up" (*2 Pet* 3:10).

Christ speaks about it and gives us signs of what will happen when it is getting near. The disciples asked him, "Tell us, when will this be, and what will be the sign of your coming and of the close of the age?" (*Matt* 24:3).

Jesus answered: "Take heed that no one leads you astray. For many will come in my name saying, 'I am the Christ', and they will lead many astray. And you will hear of wars and rumors of wars; see that you are not alarmed; for this must take place, but the end is not yet. For nation will rise against nation, and kingdom against kingdom, and there will be famines and earthquakes in various places: all this is but the beginning of the sufferings" (*Matt* 24:4-8).

The first sign will be the coming of the antichrist, people pretending to be Christ and leading many to follow him. Jesus adds: "For false Christs and false prophets will arise and show great signs and wonders, so as to lead astray, if possible, even the elect" (*Matt*

24:24). There have always been such people, often pretending to have private revelations and to have been sent by God. Already at the end of the first century, St John wrote: "Children, it is the last hour; and as you have heard that antichrist is coming, so now many antichrists have come; therefore we know that it is the last hour" (*1 Jn* 2:18).

Likewise, there will always be wars, famines and earthquakes, as there have been throughout history. Our Lord goes on: "Then they will deliver you up to tribulation, and put you to death; and you will be hated by all nations for my name's sake. And then many will fall away, and betray one another, and hate one another… And because wickedness is multiplied, most men's love will grow cold. But he who endures to the end will be saved. And the gospel of the kingdom will be preached throughout the whole world, as a testimony to all nations; and then the end will come" (*Matt* 24:9-14).

If we look at these signs, we see them fulfilled to a great extent in our own day. Christians are being put to death in great numbers in a number of countries. Some 5000 Christians were martyred in 2024, ninety per cent in Nigeria alone. Christianity and Christians are under attack and being persecuted in various ways in many countries, including in the Western world. Many Christians, including Catholics, are falling away from the faith they once practised regularly. Even though the number of Catholics in the world is growing steadily due to population increase and conversions, the number attending Mass regularly in many countries is in steady decline. As Jesus says, men's love is growing cold. And certainly the gospel has been preached throughout the whole world.

Does this mean the end of the world is near? We can never say that. There have been many times in history when the situation was dire for the Church and people thought the world was about to end. The situation today is not much different from then. We should pay no attention to those who warn of the fast-approaching "end times", the "coming chastisement", etc. The Last Day will come when God wants and it could be millions of years from now. Christ said: "But of that day and hour no one knows, not even the angels of heaven, nor the Son, but the Father only" (*Matt* 24:36). Let us go on with our daily life, living calmly, striving to grow in holiness by doing the will of God and storing up treasure in heaven. God will call us to him whenever he chooses.

60 What do we know about the Last Judgment?

We profess in the Creed that Christ "will come again to judge the living and the dead". What do we know about this judgment?

In the Nicene Creed we say, "He will come again in glory to judge the living and the dead, and his kingdom will have no end." This is the Last Judgment at the end of time. The Catechism says of it: "This will be 'the hour when all who are in the tombs will hear [the Son of man's] voice and come forth, those who have done good, to the resurrection of life, and those who have done evil, to the resurrection of judgment" (*John* 5:28-29; *CCC* 1038).

Jesus himself taught:

> When the Son of man comes in his glory, and all the angels with him, then he will sit on his glorious throne. Before him will be gathered all the nations, and he will separate them one from another as a shepherd separates the sheep from the goats, and he will place the sheep at his right hand, but the goats at the left. Then the King will say to those at his right hand, 'Come, O blessed of my Father, inherit the kingdom prepared for you from the foundation of the world; for I was hungry and you gave me food... Then he will say to those at his left hand, 'Depart from me, you cursed, into the eternal fire prepared for the devil and his angels; for I was hungry and you gave me no food... And they will go away into eternal punishment, but the righteous into eternal life" (*Matt* 25:31-46).

In this judgment, all the people who have ever lived will be judged in the presence of everyone else. Naturally, those who have already died and have been judged in their particular judgment will not be judged any differently than they were before. In the Last Judgment all will see how the others were judged, so that God's justice and mercy will be made clear. The Catechism teaches: "In the presence of Christ, who is Truth itself, the truth of each man's relationship with God will be laid bare. The Last Judgment will reveal even to its furthest consequences the good each person has done or failed to do during his earthly life" (*CCC* 1039).

When the Catechism speaks about the judgment revealing "even to its furthest consequences the good each person has done or failed to do", it can be referring to the influence on others of the life of each of us long after our death. For example, if someone was instrumental in bringing a friend into the Church, and that friend brought up his children in the faith, and they in turn brought up their children as Catholics, this effect can go on for many generations. Only in the Last Judgment will we know how much our lives have influenced others for the good down the ages. It is a marvellous reality.

But at the same time, we may have influenced someone negatively, leading them away from the Church or from a virtuous life, and they in turn have done the same with others. This too can have repercussions down the ages, and we will see in the Last Judgment the harm we have done to many people. It is a sobering thought and an invitation to strive to do good to many people while we are still alive, so that this good may pass on to future generations.

The Catechism goes on: "We shall know the ultimate meaning of the whole work of creation and of the entire economy of salvation and understand the marvellous ways by which his Providence led everything towards its final end" (*CCC* 1040). In this sense, for example, we will see how, when there were wars, earthquakes, famines, widespread poverty, etc., which wreaked so much havoc at a given time, God brought much good out of them.

Also, "The Last Judgment will reveal that God's justice triumphs over all the injustices committed by his creatures and that God's love is stronger than death" (*CCC* 1040). It may be that someone on earth was dishonest and greedy and became wealthy by cheating others, and yet seemed to enjoy all the good things of life, while someone else was very kind and generous but seemed to have no end of suffering. In the final judgment it will be seen how the first one was punished and the second rewarded. Here we are reminded of the parable of Dives, the rich man who ignored the poor man at his gate and ended up in hell, and Lazarus, the poor man who went to heaven (cf. Luke 16:19-31). If in some situations it seems that there is no justice on earth, we will see in the Last Judgment how God's justice always prevails.

Also, Christ himself was misjudged by men on earth and was sentenced to the horrible death of crucifixion, but in the Last Judgment it will be he who will come to sit in judgement on those who judged him so unjustly.

61 What do we mean by the resurrection of the body?

When our body is reunited with the soul at the end of time, do we know anything about what it will be like?

We express the truth of the resurrection of the body in the Apostles' Creed: "I believe in ... the resurrection of the body". The *Catechism of the Catholic Church* explains: "In death, the separation of the soul from the body, the human body decays and the soul goes to meet God, while awaiting its reunion with its glorified body. God, in his almighty power, will definitively grant incorruptible life to our bodies by reuniting them with our souls, through the power of Jesus' Resurrection" (*CCC* 997).

The reason why God ordained that the body should be reunited with the soul is simply that the human person is incomplete when the soul is separated from the body. By our nature, body and soul are united substantially to form one person. We are not like angels, who are pure spirits without a material body, nor like animals, which have a material body but no spiritual soul. Humans have both a body and a soul, which were made for each other and make up one person.

As St Thomas Aquinas puts it, the soul has an essential tendency, a potency, to inform a body (cf. *STh, Suppl.*, q. 70, art. 1). The soul was not meant to exist on its own without a body. It informs a body from the conception of the person until death, when the soul leaves the body. The soul then exists on its own until the resurrection of the body, when it will once again be united to the body and the person will be made whole.

So what do we know about the resurrection of the body at the end of time? The Catechism explains that the bodies of *all* will rise: "All the dead will rise, 'those who have done good, to the resurrection of life, and those who have done evil, to the resurrection of judgment'" (*John* 5:29; *CCC* 998). This is fitting. Just as our body shared in our good deeds on earth, getting tired through hard work, feeling hungry through our fasting, etc., so it is fitting that the body should share with the soul in the eternal reward of heaven. Similarly, the body also participated in many of our evil deeds, through such sins as gluttony, drunkenness, impurity, etc., and so it is fitting that the body should share in the eternal punishment of those in hell.

As regards when the body will rise, the Catechism teaches: "*When?* Definitively 'at the last day', 'at the end of the world.' Indeed, the resurrection of the dead is closely associated with Christ's Parousia: 'For the Lord himself will descend from heaven, with a cry of command, with the archangel's call, and with the sound of the trumpet of God. And the dead in Christ will rise first'" (*1 Thess* 4:16; *CCC* 1001).

At this point we might ask what the risen body will be like when it is reunited with the soul? First, it will be the same body we have now. This is a dogma of faith. The Fourth Lateran Council (1215) declared: "They will arise with their bodies which they have now" (*D* 429).

Second, the body will be free from any defects it may have had on earth. St Thomas Aquinas teaches: "Man will rise again without any defect of human nature, because as God founded human nature without a defect, even so will he restore it without defect" (*STh, Suppl.*, q. 81, art. 1). As a consequence, physical disabilities the person may have had on earth, like blindness, deafness, etc., will have no effect in the risen body. In my book *Dying to Live*, there is an account of an elderly woman who had a near-death experience in which her soul hovered above her body, watching the efforts to resuscitate her.

After she was revived she told one of the doctors how she had seen his pen fall out of his pocket and how he had gone over toward the window to pick it up. The doctor was amazed because this had in fact happened, but the woman was unconscious at the time. What was even more extraordinary was that the woman was blind, yet with her separated soul she could see (p. 31).

Also, as we have seen, following on from St Thomas' teaching that the body will rise with the greatest natural perfection is his belief that it will rise in a youthful state. This is not an official teaching of the Church, but it is at least plausible.

Finally, the risen body will be a spiritual body, not be a physical one. Perhaps this is a difficult concept to grasp. We know what physical bodies are, because we all have one, but what on earth, or in heaven, is a spiritual body? St Paul writes of it: "So it is with the resurrection of the dead. What is sown is perishable, what is raised is imperishable. It is sown in dishonour, it is raised in glory. It is sown in weakness, it is raised in power. It is sown a physical body, it is raised a spiritual body. If there is a physical body, there is also a spiritual body" (*1 Cor* 15:42-44). This is borne out when persons who have died later appear on earth, persons like Our Lady, some saints, souls in purgatory and others. They always appear in a spiritual body, recognisable but spiritual.

As regards the qualities of the spiritual body, St Paul teaches that Jesus Christ "will change our lowly body to be like his glorious body" (*Phil* 3:21). In view of this, the Scholastic theologians have agreed that the risen body will have four qualities:

1. *Incorruptibility*, not subject to decay or suffering

2. *Subtility*, or spirituality, like the risen body of Christ, which emerged from the closed tomb and passed through closed doors

3. *Agility*, like that of the risen Christ, who could suddenly appear and disappear

4. *Brightness*, filled with beauty and radiance, like the body of Christ in the Transfiguration (cf. *Matt* 17:2). Only the souls in heaven have this quality.

62 Were some of the dead really raised when Christ died on the cross?

When Christ died on the cross, St Matthew says that tombs were opened and people who had died were raised and went into the city and appeared to many. How are we meant to understand this? Did they really rise in their bodies and walk around again?

The passage to which you refer says that when Christ breathed his last, "behold, the curtain of the temple was torn in two, from top to bottom; and the earth shook, and the rocks were split; the tombs also were opened, and many bodies of the saints who had fallen asleep were raised, and coming out of the tombs after his resurrection they went into the holy city and appeared to many" (*Matt* 27:51-53).

The Navarre Bible commentary says that this passage is not clarified by any other passages in Scripture, nor has there been any statement from the Magisterium, but that the great Church writers have proposed three possible explanations.

The first is that, rather than resurrections in the strict sense, they would have been apparitions of these deceased people. This explanation, however, seems less faithful to the text, which uses the word "raised", *surrexerunt*, or "resurrected" in Latin. This implies a true resurrection of the whole person, body and soul, not just an apparition.

The second is that these people would have risen from the dead in the strict sense, in their body and soul, as did Lazarus, and would have gone on to continue living until they died again.

The third is that their resurrection would have been definitive, or glorious, in the sense that they would not need to die again, in this way anticipating the final resurrection of the body. This explanation, however, is difficult to reconcile with the clear affirmation of Scripture that Christ was the first-born from the dead (cf. *1 Cor* 15:20; *Col* 1:18).

For these reasons writers like St Augustine, St Jerome and St Thomas Aquinas prefer the second explanation, because they consider that it fits best with the sacred text and it does not present the theological difficulties of the third explanation. It is also the solution proposed by the *Catechism of the Council of Trent*.

St Thomas deals with the question in his *Summa Theologiae*, III, q. 53, art. 3, making reference to both St Augustine and St Jerome. He begins by quoting St Paul: "But in fact Christ has been raised from the dead, the first fruits of those who have fallen asleep" (*1 Cor* 15:20).

He goes on to distinguish two kinds of resurrection. The first is what he calls imperfect resurrection, where a person is raised from the dead only to die again, like Lazarus. The second is perfect resurrection, where the person is raised immortal and remains forever in life, like Christ himself, as in *Romans* 6:9: "Christ rising from the dead dies now no more."

St Thomas concludes that if Christ was the first-born from the dead in a perfect resurrection, all those who were raised before him, including those who came out of the tombs after his death, had an imperfect resurrection. They rose in their bodies and lived on earth until they died again. St Thomas says of these that "by an imperfect resurrection, some others have risen before Christ, so as to be a kind of figure of his resurrection".

The *Catechism of the Council of Trent*, or *Roman Catechism*, echoes this teaching: "These words of the Apostle are to be understood of a perfect resurrection, by which we are raised to an immortal life and are no longer subject to the necessity of dying. In this resurrection Christ the Lord holds the first place. For if we speak of resurrection, that is, of a return to life subject to the necessity of again dying, many were thus raised from the dead before Christ, all of whom, however, were restored to life to die again. But Christ the Lord, having subdued and conquered death, so arose that he could die no more, according to this most clear testimony: 'Christ rising again from the dead, dies now no more; death shall no more have dominion over him'" (*Rom* 6:9; *Roman Catechism* I, 5).

63 What do we know about the "new heaven and new earth"?

What is meant in the Bible by the expression "new heaven and new earth"? Will it be some sort of paradise here on earth?

We find the first mention of a new heaven and a new earth in the prophet Isaiah: "For behold, I create new heavens and a new earth; and the former things shall not be remembered or come into mind" (*Is* 65:17). St Peter speaks in the same vein: "Since all these things are thus to be dissolved, what sort of persons ought you to be in lives of holiness and godliness, waiting for and hastening the coming of the day of God, because of which the heavens will be kindled and dissolved, and the elements will melt with fire! But according to his promise we wait for new heavens and a new earth in which righteousness dwells" (*2 Pet* 3:11-13). The expression appears again in the last book of the Bible, the book of Revelation: "Then I saw a new heaven and a new earth; for the first heaven and the first earth had passed away, and the sea was no more" (*Rev* 21:1).

Jesus himself had said: "Heaven and earth will pass away but my words will not pass away" (*Matt* 24:35). Even though at the end of time the universe in its present form will pass away, in some way it will be renewed. The Second Vatican Council declared:

> The Church ... will receive her perfection only in the glory of heaven, when will come the time of the renewal of all things. At that time, together with the human race, the universe itself, which is so closely related to man and which attains its destiny through him, will be perfectly re-established in Christ (*LG* 48).

And the Catechism teaches: "Sacred Scripture calls this mysterious renewal, which will transform humanity and the world, 'new heavens and a new earth.' It will be the definitive realisation of God's plan to bring under a single head 'all things in [Christ], things in heaven and things on earth" (*Eph* 1:10; *CCC* 1043).

Summing up, the Catechism says: "The visible universe, then, is itself destined to be transformed, 'so that the world itself, restored to its original state, facing no further obstacles, should be at the service of the just,' sharing their glorification in the risen Jesus Christ" (St Irenaeus, *Adv. Haeres.* 5, 32, 1; *CCC* 1047).

How this will take place remains a mystery: "We know neither the moment of the consummation of the earth and of man, nor the way in which the universe will be transformed. The form of this world, distorted by sin, is passing away, and we are taught that God is preparing a new dwelling and a new earth in which righteousness dwells, in which happiness will fill and surpass all the desires of peace arising in the hearts of men" (*CCC* 1048; *GS* 39 §1).

The Church does not go into any detail about what this new state of the universe might be like. What we can be sure of, nonetheless, is that the persons there with their resurrected spiritual bodies will still be in heaven, contemplating God and all the others there. They will be focussing on God, not on each other or on the new world around them. As with so many aspects of life after death, we will find out when we get there.

It is in this final state of the universe that Christ will most perfectly reign. The Catechism teaches: "At the end of time, the Kingdom of God will come in its fullness. Then the just will reign with Christ for ever, glorified in body and soul, and the material universe itself will be transformed. God will then be 'all in all' in eternal life" (*1 Cor* 15:28; *CCC* 1060).

www.ingramcontent.com/pod-product-compliance
Lightning Source LLC
Chambersburg PA
CBHW050553160426
43199CB00015B/2649